WHAT I

"This book reveals pain and heartache at levels beyond the human experience and yet the wisdom shared and revealed is profound and uplifting. This book is for anyone who is healing the heart, emotionally or spiritually. Ms. Smith captures the human spirit and allows the reader to reflect and explore their inner fears, sadness, and truth and in the end offers hope. Take the journey to explore your own intimate crossroad through Bernadette's. A must read for anyone who has experienced sadness and loss around a relationship. This book will bring healing to any wounded heart."

– **Rev. Gordon McGregor**, Director of Development and Community Outreach, Nantucket AIDS Network, MA

"Bernadette is a scribe for the collective experience. The journal sheds light along the spiritual journey even at its darkest hour. In these pages is a piece of all of us."

– **Jackie Manning**, Cheshire, CT

"*Bernadette's Pages* is an intense journey . . . Through her courageous insights and divine messages, I was led to self-examine my own core negative beliefs. By repeated examples, she reminds one to ask: Am I operating my life from fear? What if I chose love now – how would my life, my relationships be different? *Bernadette's Pages* will change your perspective on life just as it did mine. It is truly Divinely inspired and beautifully written."

– **Dr. Kathryn L. Lawson, D.C.**, Wholistic Chiropractor, Decatur, GA

"This book is a must read . . . a beacon for your own personal journey of discovery. Whether you feel compelled to stay or are contemplating leaving, this book will open your eyes."

– **Ron D. Simmons**, Detective, Charlotte, NC

"Bernadette has the ability to get her inner voice down on paper. She clearly demonstrates how to bring journaling to the next level. What a wonderful tool for individuals seeking inner peace and successful relationships."

– **Devra Ursem-Phillips**, Visions Unlimited Coaching, Covington, GA

"Bernadette will take you on her journey from heartache to triumphant renewal, providing intimate insights into self empowerment and listening to divine guidance through the emotional chaos."

– **Suzanne DeMarchi**, Cheshire, CT

Bernadette's Pages
an intimate crossroad

Bernadette Rose Smith

published by
ENLIGHTENED INK
Covington, Georgia

Copyright ©2006 by Bernadette Rose Smith

All rights reserved. No part of this book may be reproduced or transmitted in any form or by any means, electronic or mechanical, including photocopying, recording, or by any information storage and retrieval system, without permission in writing from the publisher.

Cover art ©2006 by Ray Smith
Cover and interior design by Bernadette Smith

Published by Enlightened Ink
P.O. Box 2849
Covington, Georgia 30015

If you are unable to order this book from your
local bookseller, you may order from our website at:

www.enlightenedink.com

For information on appearance, workshop or lecture availability
please contact Bernadette through Enlightened Ink.

Library of Congress Control Number: 2006921453

ISBN 0-9777990-1-8

Manufactured in the United States of America

First Edition: June 2006

DEDICATION

*Lovingly dedicated to the memory of Rosemary J. Warner.
An angel to many, you are missed.*

GRACE

There have been many who have touched my spirit, certainly more than I could ever acknowledge here. Some have come in like gentle spring breezes, depositing fragrant gifts of insight and inspiration, while passing through on their way to someplace else. Others have come in like claps of thunder, jolting me with not so gentle two-by-four wake up calls. I am grateful to all of them for their gifts of remembering.

Then there are those who reside like the sun at the very core of life in my universe, easily finding their way into the depths of my heart. I cannot imagine a time before them. I cannot imagine a time after them. They are a part of the miracle of passage in this book. They are a part of the miracle of love in this life.

And so, with deep appreciation, I would like to say thank you:

- To God. For the whisper planted deep within my soul, helping me remember that in Your Love is my freedom. In Your Love is my home.
- To my Angels and Spiritual Teachers who make themselves known in my heart and on these pages. For their patience, peace, and gentle guidance.
- To Ray, my beloved husband and best teacher. For not balking when we came to our most challenging lesson, and for his continued commitment to healing through this relationship. I am humbled by the miracle we share. For encouraging me to share these pages, and for meeting me in every phase of this manuscript's process with whatever was needed to get it to the next stage – cover art included! For his gift of moving me in directions I wouldn't normally go.

MORE GRACE

- To Mom. For the spiritual partnership we share. She was the first true light I saw in this world and has never dimmed. She inspires me with her strength, faith, and unconditional love.
- To Dad. A man of few words, whose love and deep concern for his family shows through his actions. I am grateful for the wisdom, strength, and steadfast support he expresses on behalf of each of us.
- To Irene. For sharing her son, her life, and her love, even when our worlds turned upside down.
- To the circle of extraordinary women who loved me through the events on these pages: Sandra, Lenora, Nancy, Toni, Linda, Pam, Evelyn, Chris, Beverly, and my beautiful sisters, Peggy and Suzanne. I am blessed by their incredible spirits.
- To Chuck and Jeff. For opening their hearts and being such good listeners.
- To Debra. For loving, supporting, and *not* letting me slack off in getting these pages out there.
- To Sandra. For sharing her insight as a therapist through the healing *and* editing process. Who would have thought?
- To LaTrelle. For perching on my shoulder with her red pen through the final editing. The angels called and she heard.
- To Dale and Connie. I couldn't ask for two more patient and loving friends to show me how to bring these pages into the design phase.

And for those I have never met but whose work and words
have touched my heart and lifted my world in the best of ways:

- To *A Course In Miracles*, Kenneth and Gloria Wapnick, Marianne Williamson, Julia Cameron, dr. michael ryce, and Seth. For their insights that became a part of my road map to healing.
- To Oprah Winfrey. For reminding me of my better self and for encouraging all of us to light up the world.
- To Stevie Wonder. For our song, mine and Ray's: *Ribbon in the Sky*. It captures beautifully the moment when the miracle of love is revealed and moves us to gratitude every time we hear it.

Bernadette's Pages
an intimate crossroad

WHY THESE PAGES

    Somewhere, in the months prior to these pages, I found myself drawn to stories where ordinary people experienced an extraordinary "knowing," the kind of knowing that illuminated a serious accident or the precise moment a loved one passed on. To be struck by this sense – beyond reason – was remarkable to me. Certainly, I believed it possible to love someone in such a way that time and space imposed no limits. But could that be possible for me? As if prodded by some invisible presence, I would catch myself gazing at my husband, wondering if we shared that kind of connection. Wondering what it would take for me to "know."

    The answer came in pieces and puzzling flashes in the winter of my thirty-ninth year. Grief. Was that grief? But what was it for? Sadness. Foreboding. How could this be? Flash. Flash again. In the grocery store. Making the bed. Incredible flashes. Like lightning striking me down.

    As the pieces came together, they gave birth to questions yet unasked, but apparent like bits of broken glass reflecting in the sun. Where did they come from? What did they mean?

    The events that were about to unfold would challenge everything I believed about myself and every yardstick I used for measuring the world around me. It was one of the most painful – and perversely exciting – times of my life. I could not get through it fast enough and yet, today, I gratefully savor every memory – the way I would one of my grandmother's chocolate chip cookies.

    This is my journal from that time. Pages intended for my eyes only. They expose me. My husband. My marriage. But mostly, they expose me. There are many passages I would like to omit, but that would be less than honest. My persistent flair for the dramatic, the pity parties, the woe-is-me's, the tiresome anger and relentless questions remain because they were a necessary part of my process. Is there anyone in pain who can ask, "Why?" only once – and be satisfied with the answer? Certainly not me.

When answers broke free on these pages, words written by my hand but seeming to come from a source greater than myself, I was skeptical – and oddly relieved. Someone was listening. Someone cared enough to respond, to guide me through this time when my husband – the man to whom I had been married for almost half my life – seemed a stranger and deaf to my distress.

I hesitate to label the writings channeled or attach an identity to the authors because I do not want to limit your experience with these pages. Suffice it to say that it took this particular pain for me to let go, turn to divine guidance, and receive help at a level that I did not know existed for me. In my pain, I became teachable and, in that, was gifted the most profound learning experience I have ever had. Profoundly conscious and profoundly conscientious.

Somewhere in the process of writing for my life and sanity, between these pages and my own lamenting, a miracle was unfolding. Events, meditations, and synchronicities began to weave a pattern for healing and forgiveness, for another way to live through an experience that so many give witness to everyday.

Peace came in the writing. It was my antidote for a pain that went far deeper than I knew. Everything that lay between myself and God was being stripped away. All the busywork. The distractions. Even my husband. All the false gods. The gap was closing between me and a God I had not really trusted – one that was busy tending to others less fortunate. My distorted twist on the old adage, "God helps those who help themselves," called to surface. In the emptiness I experienced an intimacy that I had never allowed myself to know. My need to be strong and self-sufficient melted into a Presence that loved me beyond comprehension.

I have prayed earnestly for the courage to follow through on getting this book into your hands and for guidance, while editing, to keep its essence intact. Amazingly, in most of my journal entries, not only had I recorded dates, but actual times. (Not all that typical for me, especially given the circumstances.) Divinely guided – no doubt – and, believe me, I am grateful. It made the compilation of this material possible.

I have chosen to retain the intimacy of the journal format. In this way, you will be present with me as the story unfolds. Months act as chapters. Dates, times, and headings introduce the nature of the passages. "Spirit Dialog" introduces channeled writing, with Spirit's response in italics. "In the Margins" introduces the passages where I failed to enter a date or time. You will also see places for your own writing, should you feel inspired to join in.

So, why am I offering these pages? Because I hope they will encourage you to look beyond the obvious and find your own miracle when life challenges you, or someone you love, to the edge. And because I believe they offer a gift that was meant to be shared – from the very beginning.

BRS

THE SET UP

How much background do you need to grasp the story about to unfold? And what will only serve to muddy the waters? Should I ease you in, toes first? Or let you do a belly smacker, catching your breath as you go?

This is not a novel. I will not be able to politely introduce you to all the characters or tell you their histories. Reading these pages will feel more like eavesdropping, at first. With the edginess that comes when you stumble within earshot of what you recognize immediately is a very private conversation, an edginess loaded with questions. Stressful until you get your bearings, until you settle into the rhythm of what you are overhearing.

So, how do I help you get your bearings more quickly and keep you turning the pages? Keep you moving past any discomfort you may feel about the questions that will naturally occur?

Perhaps all you need is already in the writings. And yet, I can't resist feeling that certain details are significant – even necessary. That my husband and I shared eighteen years of marriage appears, at first thought, to be fairly important. But to go on to share that he and I were best friends and had always enjoyed an exceptional level of communication, seems not only a contradiction but a blatant fabrication in contrast to the pages to come. How, you might justifiably ask, considering these significant details, could two people be so blind?

The temptation to dig in and analyze, justify, or "soften the blow" is strong and leads me to wonder at what point do I stop? So, I have decided to lighten up, step out of the way, and imagine how my angels would set up our story. This directive keeps popping into my head: Let's see where *they* want to take it.

Once upon a time, in a land far, far away, there lived a young man and a young woman. Her name was Bernadette. His was Ray. They entered their worlds with a fairly standard assortment of challenges and lessons to learn. Bernadette, the oldest of five children, began her life as an Army brat, moving from place to place before graduating into the world feeling different and lonely. Ray, an only child and nine years older, began his life living in a small town before graduating into the world feeling different and lonely.

Magical sparks flew when first they met and, as their sense of isolation melted away, took no time at all in mounting to intoxicating flames of purpose for each other. Like a melody awakening a long forgotten verse, their spirits embraced with absolute faith as their first date in March led to wedding bells in June.

They struck out in search of their kingdom on a journey to uncover the treasure they had found. A time of comfort and joy was given, two years in the Big Apple – New York City – to be exact, with challenges, ever so faintly whispering from the darkened edges of their awareness.

But alas, this honeymoon would not go on forever, for they had much to do. They found themselves transported back to their meeting place. Back to their roots. In so doing, they took on their baggage and all the challenges that implies. They weathered many a storm together. Everything from A to Z. All the good stuff that brings any self respecting couple to their knees and to their God.

We were there, with The Comforter and The Spirit Helpers, to lead them through the next most dangerous phase. To help them remember. Would Ray and Bernadette do the work? Would they honor their holy agreement or be lost to each other in a world of pain and guilt, with no forgiveness in their hearts?

In the time known as August the thirteenth of 1993, in response to a question posed, The Spirit Helpers broke through onto the pages of Bernadette's journal, writing . . .

"Desire is that which sends you Home, that which lets you know that you are wanted to be Home. Your question is of a sexual nature, in this plane, because that is your perceived point of concern.

God does want you to be Home. You seek that knowledge in your imagined sexual ecstasy. You feel lost and want that completion. Your ego interprets it as physical but your need is in spirit from where you feel a break."

When she went on to express her fears about her beloved's depression, and his lost desire and passion for her, They gave her a signal of what was to come.

"What he feels, or does not feel, is not a reflection of you at this time. Nor is it a sign that your Father no longer desires your entrance into the heavenly realm. Do not fear this nor the emptiness you think you will feel.

Do not look to Ray to know that you are wanted. He is in a slump. Give him the space to be loosened from that which weights him down. The heaviness you feel from him contrasts the radiance he is. Do not give up on him. He needs you to be light. That is your purpose with him. The way may not be easy for you in respect to this, but you knew that from the beginning of this arrangement.

He may need to find another woman, to spark his passion again, to see you anew. He sees you through old eyes and thus he does not see you at all, for that person no longer is in existence. You are invisible to him. Do not fault him for this. His load is much heavier than yours and his task is not just for himself. You must not walk away in frustration. He will not renege on the arrangement.

Remain calm and detached. Your ecstasy is still for him because he does give that back to you. Another is not to experience your surrender. That would leave you empty. He does indeed fill you. Know this and remain true. All is necessary and as it should be."

Though she grasped the earnestness of these words, she took them metaphorically. Her pain and fear would not let her see. The Spirit Helpers broke through once again, shortly before her thirty-ninth birthday in the following year:

"There is much to be done. You have been working very hard to make adjustments in this plane. You fight yourself. You still do not trust Ray to come through for you. You think his desire for you cannot be revived. It is a 'little' desire that you want, but this 'little' desire is not what you need. It is much too little to last. He will find you desirable in a way he has never known.

You and he are working in different realms. Keep yourself busy until he is through. Channel your sexual energy until then. You can use it to open up, to hear us more clearly. It is as simple as being clear on what you would intend to happen to the energy.

Do not be concerned that you don't remember. There is an aspect of yourself that does, and will take over. It is getting closer for the next major shift."

When it came to pass, literally, as The Spirit Helpers had indicated, a foundation for trust was put in place – a critical foundation for Bernadette and ultimately for Ray, as you will now come to witness.

End of the once upon a time. We welcome you to Bernadette's pages.

MARCH

FALLING • JOURNAL • Thursday Morning, March 3

    Missed a day in my journal and a hell of a one at that. Now I know what those incredible waves of sadness were about on my flight back from the gift show in New York. Why I felt like crying when the plane landed. The weird irritation that surfaced when Ray picked me up at the terminal. He felt like a stranger. Distant, in a way I couldn't put my finger on. And the cats! My God, all the neighbors' cats perching on our front porch – strolling down our sidewalk – when we got back from the airport that night. Now I know why it struck me as so odd that they not be in their own yards. Significantly surreal. And this anger I've felt at Ray's vanishing act when Suzanne came into town on business last weekend. Not meeting us for dinner. Getting home after she left. He's never been that way with family. Totally out of character. Distracted and inattentive – for weeks. It finally makes sense. Last night when he said we needed to talk, all the foreboding came flooding in. I was devastated. Even before he confessed to wanting a separation. To there being another woman. And right now I feel so crazy with it – I just want to die!

    I can't imagine being without him. We've been through so much together. I'm willing to bet this *other* woman would have bailed out on him years ago! God, you saved us for this? When I called my friend Samantha, she said I needed to let go of Ray and let You handle it. He's made up his mind. So it seems that is all I *can* do – let go and get on with my life. But how do I do that when so much of my life was *our* life?

    I can't compete with this woman! She has a clean slate. An untarnished mirror. He can look into her eyes and see a new man – a new life reflected back.

God, can't we rise above this? Is this what it's about – struggle and loss? I do not accept that we aren't good for each other. And yet, I feel so absolutely helpless. The control freak has freaked out. There is nothing left.

What a mess. How does he think he's going to make this happen? We're barely able to pay our bills *now*. What do I do? Decide what is best for me – that's what. I don't want to lose him. Should I let him stay here – stalling – hoping for a reconciliation – until our finances are neat and tidy? No. That's a bad idea. I'm not giving that to her. If she gets him, she gets him with *all* the baggage!

Okay, so if I tell him to get out now – what if he moves in with her? God, I can't stand the thought that the last time we made love was the last time. If I force him to leave, I might lose any chance of winning back his heart. But then if he stays here – with me acting weird and insecure and angry and God knows what all – hell, I will give him even more reasons to hate me. I can't do that to myself, either.

So, what *is* best for me?

That he should love me! God, I've *been* changing and yet he doesn't see anything but the past. How can I compete with her, carrying that load?

Damn! I can't believe he had an affair – and that he fell in love with her – *six years ago!* How did I miss that? Should I feel grateful that she backed out? That she married someone else? And now, after all this time has passed, he decides to call her – for what? And to see her while I was out of town – on *my* birthday!

He says she's divorced and still has feelings for him. That he doesn't want to lose his second chance at a "once in a lifetime" love! What the *hell* is that! What possessed him to make that call?

"For the thing which I greatly feared is come upon me."[*] Maybe I invited this in when we argued – not that

[*]Book of Job 3:25

long ago – and I drew a parallel between Ray and my first love, Matthew. I remember crying when I said he was starting to "feel like Matthew" to me.

Matt and I were so close. We were sensitive. Artistic. Expressive. Real creative cohorts. I think everyone expected us to get married. I know I did. We seemed perfect for each other. Perfectly sick. When I look back on the patterns, the codependency, I can see we were doomed. But I didn't see it then. When Matthew announced that he wanted to date other women – it felt just as abrupt and shocking as this with Ray.

Am I so dense? Here it is again – only now, with eighteen years of marriage behind me!

Dammit. Ray probably can't even remember our good times. The interests we share. Interests that have created a history of spiritual beliefs and revelations, artistic ventures and brainstorming, jaunts to the mountains, books, plays, music venues. What worked between us lost in a blur – seven years of our marriage – lost. Wiped out because he was too damn busy hiding and controlling his drinking to notice what we had to be grateful for. And now, after all this time in sobriety, all he can do is focus on how sick he thinks *I am*? Is this what he really wanted to see all along?

Okay. I don't know what it's like to have his struggles. Maybe it was hard for him – numbing out like that for so many years – believing that was the only way he could get through life. But now that his feelings have come to – he takes them elsewhere? God, I'm scared. What can save us? I want to beat this but I can't make him feel for me. I can't even get him to *see* me!

If I let him stay here for *any* length of time, I need to know he's working on our marriage. He cannot see her. She is that "drink," and he has to abstain!

Who am I kidding? He's not in a place where he can do that. I've been there. I know the signs. I might have opted for the other guy, had Ray found out and given me an ultimatum. The illusion of a fresh, clean start can be so damn tempting. A shortcut to a new you without all the painful and tedious inner work. A chance to "pretty up" and escape in the rapture. I was looking for something I had lost – and thought I could find with another man. But, dammit, as messed up as I was, I knew those experiences were not *real* love. And I never tried to pin the blame on Ray. It was my stuff, my shortcoming. "Was" being the key word. I don't need to "act out" that way today – and haven't in years! So, why the hell is *he* doing it? Why now? Why with us in recovery?

If I confess to my past indiscretion now, am I just trying to convince him that he is making a mistake? I know I can't use my experience with another man to manipulate him, but if I don't say anything, where will he be looking from when he looks back – as I am now? And with whom? And what will he recognize as love?

God, tell me what to do! You know what I want. You know what I need. Can I trust You? I'm going to be making some pretty major decisions. Give me the strength. I've never hurt so bad! And I am really pissed off with You!

JOURNAL • Thursday Evening, March 3

Sandra agreed to see me today. I know my hysterical call last night put her in a tough spot, but I had to talk with someone and Ray suggested I call her. Maybe this isn't in accordance with the rules or code of ethics for therapists, but I don't feel our knowing each other, or her working with Ray in his depression, is a conflict. I trust her ability to be objective and non-judgmental. It's important that the person I bare my soul and my marriage to won't take sides. I got that from her in today's session. I know how hard she prayed over this last night – how all logic said to refer me to another counselor. I'm grateful that she listened to her heart and that Ray was willing to share her. We all agreed that if my seeing her proved to be a conflict of interest, she would refer me to someone else, someone she felt confident could work with me.

What a wreck I am! I feel so helpless. I've always been the strong one for others. This is sad. I don't have the will or the strength to pull it together and fake it. Thank God for friends like Lea. If she had not stayed with me today and driven me out to Sandra's office, I never would have made it.

I asked her to stop, on the way, at the salon where Emily works. I was obsessed with getting my hair cut. Wanted it all chopped off. Maybe I did it "at Ray" because he loves long hair. As a way to shock him. To show him how bad I felt. Funny, I had been toying with the idea of changing my hair for months. Nothing like being motivated into action by your husband leaving you! I have heard that, in some cultures, a woman cutting off all her hair is an act of grieving. Maybe so. It felt like it when I looked in the mirror. Face pale, eyes red from crying, dark circles under them from no sleep, and long tresses of hair on the floor around me. What a sight I must have been!

Poor Emily. We're all so close. Like family. I know it was a shock – and hard for her to do what I was asking. I caught her watery glances at Lea as each strand hit the floor. She kept asking, "Are you sure you want to do this today?" She would not cut it as short as I wanted. Said I could take more off later – and I will. I need to see someone different looking back at me in the mirror. Maybe it will be easier to put up a front.

Ray was shaken when I walked in the door after Lea dropped me off. I think it concerned him that I would do something so extreme as having my hair cut inches from my scalp. He was carefully polite. Like when you are talking someone off a ledge. He should be concerned – dammit.

We needed a neutral place to talk, so we went to the little pancake house down the street. I asked if he'd still help me with the gift show this weekend. He seemed surprised. Said of course he would, but I sensed it would cut into time he was planning on spending with *her*. Now that he has told me, he's already got one foot out the door. Like he can't wait to get away from me. He says he still loves me. Still cares about me – still wants to be in my life. Only now I have to share him with another woman?

Damn! Setting up the booth. Working the show. Breaking it all down. Can't believe I'm locked into this. It's too late to call the company and arrange for a sub. I can't do this without him but I don't know if I am strong enough to be with him – in public – without breaking down. I have to do this. I have to hold on until after the show. I can't crash now. God, I feel like I'm flying apart.

ON ANGELS' WINGS • SPIRIT DIALOG
Friday Morning, March 4

The pain is intense. I keep trying to remind myself that this is pain for what *may* come, not pain for this very second. This very second, Ray is in bed. Moments before, I lay in his arms. Awake. Trying to keep my mind from racing to the time when he will not be here.

Let go. Let go. Trust God. That's all you truly have, Bernadette. Ray has come between you and your Father because you have placed him there. All the more "seemingly justifiable" because yours is a holy relationship. But if you are to live through this pain, and we do want you to live through this pain, you must use every tool you have ever learned, to stay in the moment. And you must receive all the love and support you can from those around you, who would help you to remember what you would momentarily forget. You must keep writing. The opening is occurring. This pain is necessary to execute that which you have wanted all along. We can never know, when we ask, what we will truly receive. This is part of what you asked for, so should you not be more careful with what you think you should ask for now?

We know you wanted to dump your feelings on paper here, but nothing new would have been written this morning. More important than your knowing the connection, is your accepting the connection with us. We are here. Use all that we have given you to let us speak to you when the writing seems to be blocked. The comfort that you have with these divining tools is a comfort to know that we are here.

You will not know the outcome because that would rob you of the lesson, or alter the manner in which you walk through it.

My mind is blank. Where did they go?

We are not gone. Your ego blocked us out with fear of the outcome. Trust your Father. Give Ray to Him. Give yourself to Him. You could go no further this way, singularly nor as a couple. Drastic measures are necessary because your aspirations are high. Let go and this will greatly accelerate the lesson. It need not be long. Hold on, and the pain will be much longer, and the effect on your health will be great. You do tend to eat away at yourself, so be careful what you "Will." Cancer is not beyond your creation. That would be a sad waste, and unintended by us. So, be diligent in your thinking and in utilizing all your support.

You are not meant to leave Ray, but you must attain the Self that you truly are before any relationship in the future, as you see it, can work. You have set the standards, so you can reach them. You cannot live with falling short, nor can he. Give him this freedom. Give both of you this freedom. Trust in the best outcome.

Yes, she is a catalyst. You better let go, or she may need to remain longer. That is not a threat. You make this all up. Can you not see that all of you have your learnings and your parts? Perhaps she is someone you love dearly who would offer this gift, this challenge for you and Ray to know your true Selves. So, think on that.

Oh, we feel you fighting it. Think on it lightly. Now let it go. It is not meant to make you sick. Go in peace and dowse in your Course.* Amen.

---

*_A Course in Miracles_ (Temecula, CA, 1985, Foundation for _A Course in Miracles_)

I feel nauseous. Maybe, if I let go I can shorten this.

You can let him go, but you must not think that your "letting go" will bring the outcome you desire. There must be no strings attached to your letting go. Should your desire be attained, it will not be attained through your letting go. The only "outcome" of letting go is peace. There is no other response. It is as a reflex action. It is for your peace, and no other reason. That which would bring the desired outcome, whatever it is, is from a place you cannot remember, so you cannot understand. But surely you can understand peace?

Don't try to name the peace. Don't try to label the peace. You name it, you label it, you set limitation upon it. You think the peace you name would be the best, but it is sadly far from the peace we would give you. Remember this thought throughout the day. Don't label. Don't name. And you won't limit. Amen.

ANSWERED PRAYER • SPIRIT DIALOG
Saturday Morning, March 5

When the clock radio went off this morning, a female vocalist was singing a song that I had not really listened to before.[*] Instead of getting up right away, I lay there – focused on this woman's words and grateful for her message. It was about finding our hero. About finding the strength to survive life's difficult times. About looking for hope and knowing truth – and realizing that our hero lies inside.

I know I need to keep trying to look within. To let go of Ray – of what he will or won't be doing – and look at me and what I will or won't be doing.

Last night, I had a dream that I found a diary. It was ancient and made of stone. In it, a woman was confessing a terrible thing she'd done. She had made love to a dear friend's husband. She was deeply troubled and it was obvious that she loved both of these people very much. Suddenly it dawned on me that she was talking about us.

[*]Mariah Carey, *Hero*

Shocked, my eyes raced to the bottom of the page to see if she had signed it. The name, Catherine, appeared. At first I drew a blank. Then I realized she was the Catherine I knew from Al Anon. I was outraged at being betrayed by someone in the program. Someone I trusted. Ray came in and found me reading the tablet. I started screaming, "No!" Then I woke up.

Ray won't tell me her name. I've asked. I've asked what she looks like. Where she lives. He says knowing these things will not make me feel better, that this separation has nothing to do with her.

This morning I feel some peace. I know it won't last because it is tied to what's going on with Ray. He's on that emotional roller coaster I know all too well. Now *she* is acting weird and he's afraid he may get dumped. At the moment, he's angry. But as soon as he sees her – if she gives him any glimmer of hope – he'll be back on cloud nine. We are both so sick. Here I am focusing on him – and her – and not me. My peace is "labeled and limited" to the current thought that she may dump him and he will stay with me. How pitiful is that? A poor foundation for peace. I do see it. Maybe this is the only way that I could.

Several weeks ago, I remember asking God to speed things up. Was emphatic when I said I could not live like this any longer. Have no memory of what prompted that prayer at the time. Probably something related to my artist's block or our financial stress. I recall saying that I didn't care what it took to change – just "Let's do it and be done!"

Guess I *should* be careful what I pray for. I wonder if that was the same day Ray felt compelled to find her. I know he wasn't making it up when he told me that his compulsion to call her came "out of the blue." What a strange dialog that must have been when he argued that he didn't know her number and the inner voice asked where she worked? All he could remember was that she used to work at a hospital. Said the voice directed him to look in the phone book and assured him he would recognize the name of the hospital when he saw it. When he did, he said he threw the book down and thrashed around the room. Don't know if I buy that part – but I do believe he felt like a man possessed.

This other woman is very likely God's answer to my prayer, though I'm sure, by now, Ray believes she is the answer to *his*! He's been miserable in his struggle with depression. It's evident. I know that he is steadily praying and writing – just like I am. I have to believe that, if this is God's answer – to either prayer – I can handle it.

I need to stop trying to figure out how God is going to fix this – wondering whose prayer is being answered – second guessing what every twist and turn means in the big picture. I really want to know peace from the *inside*. Not resulting from Ray or his actions. I love him deeply, but I have to let go and let God move me through this process without constantly looking over His shoulder.

I was hoping they would take over my writing this morning but even though they haven't, I feel their presence.

You see how you think? You are constantly second guessing in all your affairs. As you meditate, to get quiet, you race ahead to the gift show today. Amid all this emotional turmoil, you become mentally busy. If you could be aware and stop this meandering, we could reach you more often.

Look on this. You not only second guess with Ray now. He is but one avenue by which you question God and try to control with your thinking. You need more empty spaces! Amen.

Ouch!

HOW DARE HE • JOURNAL
Sunday, 3:00 a.m., March 6

I'm drinking a cup of valerian tea, hoping that I can get back to sleep. Slept for two hours. The terrible burning that's been in the pit of my stomach for the past couple days has dissolved into a trembling between my stomach and my heart. The overlapping physical and emotional sensations are very strange. The burning feels like fear boring right through my stomach, while the trembling feels like mini-explosions threatening to shatter my heart. When I try to focus on calming my heart, fear races into a pure rage that merges so rapidly with pain, my heart feels as if it is being *physically wrenched* from my ribcage. I honestly feel as if it is breaking! Then the rage darts up and catches in my throat, choking me – telling me that I will soon have to find a way to give this anger, this fear a voice.

Tonight I saw Ray in a different light. I saw how screwed up he really is and how much I have placed him on a pedestal. I am so pissed off. All those years of his drinking and my not knowing! When I think of how sick I got – emotionally *and* physically – living with his alcoholism! His sneaking. Hiding. Forgetting. Messing up. And there I was giving him the benefit of the doubt. Thinking I was imagining things. Thinking I was too sensitive. He cruised through those years anesthetized, numb with alcohol, while I was seriously questioning my sanity!

Who is this man who couldn't get sober without judging me hopeless? Who couldn't live with me as I was – even for a little while – and maintain his sobriety? (So much for better or worse.) He couldn't deal with the guilt. He had to take another drink to numb out on us. *She* was his drink!

How noble of him to remain with me when *she* backed out that first time. Hell, he wasn't *with* me, committed to this relationship – but resigned because the "true love" of his life married someone else! Now I understand his hair-trigger temper. Why he couldn't see the changes I was making. He didn't want to! He wanted her to be the one. He needed her to be the one, so he could stay numb to us and the dysfunction we'd shared for so many years. She's been here all along so he could keep score and justify his choice to keep his feelings intact and away from me. All the while I was opening up and knocking down my walls, he was putting up his as fast as he could. No wonder I've been so tired. He took my efforts, my energy, and built his case. He has never given us a true chance – just resignation!

Even knowing this, I still love him.

God, I'm so mad. This hurts so bad! I know I have to get through this anger. I'm afraid to feel this. It's overwhelming. I don't want to turn it on him or me.

Damn! He's anesthetized now! Where is the divine justice in this? He'll leave and not feel the pain of separation because he has her to distract him – again! He's running. I think I got too close to being what he wanted. It was better for him when I was contemptible because he knew how to be with that. He never had to risk true intimacy. Now he is challenged. Thus his compulsion to call her after all these years. He can feel attraction, lust, passion for her and call that intimacy because it feels as if he's made a special connection – but he is disconnected!

How dare he! How dare he say he has no feelings left for me! He wants no feelings! Damn! I can't believe this is really happening. Spirit says Ray has no forgiveness for himself and so *cannot* for me. That only forgiveness can bring the shift in perception needed to allow us to work through this, to allow him to see himself as he desires to be. That this separation would not be necessary if he could forgive. That it's not about responsibility in the worldly sense that he talks of – but about responsibility for his feelings.

God, I see he can't stay with me. He's safe with her. There will be no challenge to his feeling of integrity when I'm out of the picture. He can go back to business as usual and get away with it because she makes it *look* so different. How many years will go by before he realizes the path he's chosen is no different than our sickest days together? What a paradox! Staying together only appears to be choosing more of the same because it *looks* the same. But to stay, in the face of honesty and intimacy! That would truly be different.

He won't let me love him. He won't let himself love me. She doesn't have his love either. I wonder how long before she finds that out. Maybe she will never know. Or maybe she wants the same as he. To hide. They just might live happily ever after.

Perhaps he's found himself in the same place I was when he first got sober. When I got a sense of how sick I was, in contrast to his recovery. Only thing is, I stayed and faced my issues. Now that *I'm* getting better – he turns and runs from his?

God, it's 4:12 a.m. and I'm absolutely wide awake. I cannot keep going on two hours sleep and so little food. What do I do?

IN THE MARGINS

I think I'm going to spend more time over at Lea's. She's open to it. Said I can sleep in the extra bedroom. I have to get out of here. It is too hard watching him come and go. Wondering what he's really doing. He commented that I should consider moving in with Lea or Emily. Or at least get a roommate. Do I detect that he is worried about my being alone – or is that just wishful thinking on my part?

Who will be living where? He wants to stay here for now, but said he would leave that up to me. I think he'd like for me to be the one to move out. I guess I should be grateful. At least he is not racing to move in with *her*!

CAMPING OUT • JOURNAL • Tuesday, March 8

I feel calmer, now that I have spent the night here at Lea's. Her home is very peaceful. The pain is filtered, like sunlight through smoked glass – not quite so intense. What I feel most is emptiness. And sadness for how I could allow myself to become so empty and not notice. I filled myself with Ray. Guilty of the same as he. Trying to complete myself in him, as I accuse him of doing with her.

It is so hard not to think about going home. But how can he know what it will be like without me if I'm there under his nose? I guess I have to trick myself into hoping that, in leaving him alone at the house, he might come to miss me or have second thoughts about this separation.

I'm like an addict going through withdrawal. So antsy! If I could just believe what Spirit told me on August the thirteenth, before this whole business started, I might get through it better.

I have to call Peggy and tell her what is happening before she flies in. God, less than a month ago I was with Suzanne, cutting up over margaritas, waiting for a Ray that would never show for dinner. She flew out not knowing why – not the real reason – and still doesn't. How odd, getting to see both of my sisters, almost back to back, with all this going on.

Damn. I intended to pamper Peggy and show her the town. Give her time-out from being a Mommy. I don't think I can fake it and I can't let her see me like this. What kind of sister would I be, to let her come with no warning? She loves Ray. I don't want her to see this stranger in him. I have to tell her. I have to be strong.

I don't think I can do this.

JOURNAL • Wednesday, March 9

Well, 5:21 a.m. and the anger has awakened me. At least I got six hours of restful sleep with no sleeping pills – and no nightmares! Rather than stew mentally, I'll dump my anger on the page and hopefully get back into a place of peaceful resolve so I can go on with my day.

All these things I want to say to Ray – to change *him*? I *allowed* him to pull me off my path. How could I have thought it would be satisfying, or safe, to support his dreams while mine disappeared?

How stupid! Day after day, putting in my time for that

someday when the payoff would come. When we would be free to play and express who we truly are – together – as a couple. There has been little joy for either of us in this kind of existence. He faults me that I could not lighten up. He allowed me to work a full time job – help him with his business – take care of him in so many ways. He needed me to be the heavy, then had the audacity to believe that I was capable of being no more than a caretaker! He is running as fast as he can into the arms of a woman who would be for him all that I am not? Damn. I want to play, be spontaneous, adventurous – but who has the time or energy? *He* is my chronic fatigue!

Curious that he was so insistent on getting me *The Artist's Way* when we passed the display at the bookstore.[*] How many months ago? Rather ironic, when you think about it. How I couldn't get past the chapter on "Recovering a sense of possibility." Now we *both* have our *artist's way* writings to look back on – and see how miserable we were!

But we must have had something special. Something strong. Something that defies understanding because we should never have made it eighteen years with our baggage. That is the part that hurts. That is the part I hate to turn away from. But I can't watch him go through this rebellion. Perhaps I should wonder what's wrong with me that I would love a man who could do this.

I am not angry that he is trying to become "whole and responsible." I am angry that he did not have the courage to leave and address his codependency, six years ago, after she backed out. If he believed he no longer loved me and wanted to assert his independence, he should have left then! His courage comes through another woman, not himself. And his drawing courage and strength from her to make this break, tells me that he is not truly ready to stand responsible, to be accountable. He's just shifting his weight from me to her.

[*]Julia Cameron, *The Artist's Way* (New York, 1992, G.P. Putnam's Sons)

Still, I see so much in him. I have to stop looking because it kills me to think that she might have what I never got with him. In time, the part of me that wants him back will be silent.

JOURNAL • Continued, 6:30 a.m.

Just let in Lea's kitty, Thomas. What a lover he is. Even to creatures that should be his prey. Cute, now he's trying to crawl on my lap. I think I know why Smitty is more Ray's cat, even though I'm the one attached to him. He's like Ray. And my relationship with Smitty mirrors my relationship with Ray. I worry over him, love on him with that fearful protectiveness – and yet can't *unconditionally* seek comfort from him because he is so unpredictable. One moment he's purring, the next he's hissing and swatting. That is Ray with me.

Ray says he wants to open his heart. To learn of love. But the conditions that he placed – that *we* placed – on love destroyed us and almost destroyed me. I say almost because, here at Lea's, I feel my spirit strengthening.

Dear God, please help me. When I write about this man, it's as if he were a monster. I know he's not. This man is as much a stranger to himself as he is to me. I hope he can become that whole man – and that I might still share my life with him. Keep him safe in Your arms, as I am. Thank You.

JOURNAL • Continued, 7:44 a.m.

It just occurred to me that, where Smitty is like Ray, our neighbor's cat, Little Bit, is like me. I've always felt a deep connection to her. Now I know why. She's like me looking for love. Trying to slip into a home that cannot hold her and loyal to that desire even though the love she gets is just a "little bit." Funny how we chose to name her that. Ray doesn't know, when he gives her attention and lets her sneak in, that she is like me. The feelings and tenderness he's lost for me

– shown in his expression for her. When I've been sad for her, as she looks wistfully in the window and cries at the door, I have really been sad for me. I project my pain onto her.

JOURNAL • Continued, 11:00 a.m.

God, give me some peace. I've been so blind. Now I have to treat Ray like a drug that I need to abstain from. I don't know if I can do him just a little. I don't have the strength to be with him or even hear his voice on the phone. I was in such a good place yesterday – and this morning. I felt some hope. Not so engulfed in the pain. Damn that phone call! That was my drug and now I am sliding down into the black hole again. I can't focus. I'm not clear. I don't know how much longer I can live like this, bouncing between Lea's home and mine. I can't play Ray's "roommate." I am still his wife!

JOURNAL • Continued, 1:10 p.m.

I want to be angry. Angry with Ray for coming into my life. Angry with God for saving me from other relationships, only to be rejected in this one. But I can't. The questions keep popping in. Where would I be if we had never met? Who would I be? All the moves. New York. Detroit. Atlanta. Only geographic cures? Maybe not. Each move, each place, gifted me with experiences and discoveries that revealed facets of myself that might have remained hidden. He encouraged me to take creative risks. To explore outside my safety zone. He expanded my world. He expanded me. Hell, he is doing it even now! When I look at that, I am more grateful than angry.

JOURNAL • Continued, 1:35 p.m.

I can see why it's hard to stay home. So little of me is reflected back. Ironic that he's accused me of being controlling. Most of our home reflects him! His stuff. His furniture.

His nic nacs. The part that is *me* is how I tried to arrange what was his so I could fit in – rather than add something of my own. What a sad metaphor! And I've done the same with him emotionally. I've tried to work around and arrange his emotional stuff so I could fit in, all the while feeling guilty for pushing myself on him.

As I look around, Lea's place draws me in. Somehow, I see me here. Perhaps a "me" that has disappeared? I do see a little of myself in our kitchen. How I pushed for the purple curtains and my vintage doll dishes on the little shelf over the sink! Dishes that I played with and treasured, knowing that they were once my mother's. The innocence of childhood tea parties, shared between generations. Kitchen, a room that supports nourishment. Purple, a color that supports my spiritual nature. Mom, a woman of spiritual strength – my mentor. What a powerful, subliminal message! No wonder I like that room.

I don't want to arrange someone else's stuff anymore, without adding *me* to it. That's why it hurts to stay home. I see so much of him and my "arrangings." And isn't it interesting that I find myself managing a showroom at the gift mart, arranging someone else's merchandise – with no true influence. Impotent. Not creative. Where is *my* space? Where is *my* stuff?

I remember, during our many yard sales after the move from Oxford to Chamblee, how much I kept joking about, "Whose stuff is this?" I thought I was talking about volume! Whose stuff is this? A more profoundly telling question than I realized.

JOURNAL • Continued, 2:00 p.m.

Yesterday, I walked barefoot through the leaves and ate chicken soup sitting on the broken rock wall down by the old fountain. This morning I sat cross-legged on the rug in Lea's bathroom, in front of her full length mirror. All my make-up spilled out on the floor, like a toy box dumped over. Feeling like a little girl at play. A pixie with a new short haircut, looking back at me in the mirror, painting over her "look what you've done to me" face. On my way home, tonight, I will treat myself to a potted hyacinth – to place by my side of the bed. And in the morning I will pick daffodils from our backyard, for a bouquet that will remind me of sunshine yellow days to come.

God, help me to be in the moment and grasp that which has beauty and gives pleasure. Help me to be grateful for the goodness still present in my life.

JOURNAL • Continued, 2:30 p.m.

These past few years, so many of my yardsticks have been taken away. Everything I have used to tell me who I was or that I was okay. My home. My possessions. My belief systems. Is this marriage just another thing I am to relinquish? Eighteen years may be the longest time I will ever share with one man. Almost half my life, up to this date. I thought, when we exchanged our vows, that our foundation would be solid.

Did God join us, or was it something else? So many friends have shared with me that Ray and I were their inspiration, their beacon for the possibility of a true and lasting relationship. When they lost hope, they looked to us. How sad. We were their yardstick. How one shift touches so many!

JOURNAL • Continued, 3:45 p.m.

There is an odd calmness coming over me. I feel as if something, or someone, is literally prying me open and rearranging my mind. Something is being dramatically altered. What I am seeing now, I can't quite describe. I'm struck by the complexity of events and information. So much is being pointed out to me. Ordinary things with an extraordinary purpose, overlapping and restructuring. Am I imagining this?

BACK HOME • JOURNAL • Thursday, March 10

I still feel calm this morning, even though I am back at the house with Ray. Maybe I'm just numb. I now know that I can live here alone. I know we can't go back, that I don't want him this way. This other woman is not so much a factor, nor is his rejection of me. I find myself focused more on how we have related through the years.

I'm uncomfortable with this lack of feeling for him. I feel a distaste for his activities, as he chatters on about his acting and "stuff." Like he really does need to grow up, as he says, but he is still just talking about it. I know he thinks, because I'm in this calmer space, we can go back to business as usual until he is ready to leave.

Holy Spirit, give me the right words to say this morning. I will give him one more chance to reconcile. If he doesn't go for it, I am asking him to move out. I think he has a session with Sandra today, so he can work through this with her.

Tonight I'll pick up Peggy from the airport. I'm grateful for her desire to come regardless of the circumstances. She was so clear when she said to forget my big sister stuff and asked if I wanted her to be here. It cut right through all my shit. All I could say was "Yes." It was as if she read my mind and knew my fear when she said, "Good. Don't worry about being strong. Let me take care of *you* for a change." Thank you, Peggy. You may never know how much that meant.

IN THE MARGINS

Holy Spirit gave me the words to say to Ray this morning. No reconciliation. I guess I already knew that, but I had to try. He will be moving out as soon as he can find a place.

JOURNAL • Continued, 10:45 a.m.

I am in the showroom with a feeling I do not understand. I'm obsessed with a desire to make love to Ray, one more time. Not to win him back. Not to compete with what they've found. I only want to be *us* – perfectly in the moment, making love. No past. No future. And God, I don't understand why!

This is crazy. I don't need this right now! I have tried calling Lea, Sandra, Samantha – everyone is unreachable. So why, *why* do I have this feeling? I was really hoping for a calm day and now I'm just as agitated as I was yesterday.

JOURNAL • Continued, 11:15 a.m.

Perhaps I've never made love to Ray, absolutely in the present moment. Maybe I have. But so many of the recent years I've gotten lost in fantasy. With him in mind – but fantasy none the less.

That he has been with another woman is no more pertinent to me now than my having been with another man. Can I make love, and feel love, in the present? What would that be like? Absolutely *present* in the present. No fantasies. No distractions. Just him and me, face to face, eye to eye, soul to soul.

Right, like that could be possible. Especially now. I couldn't stand to risk any more rejection.

JOURNAL • Continued, 1:25 p.m.

Just finished lunch. French fries and a cup of coffee. Tried calling Sandra again, to see if I could set an appointment for tomorrow. The receptionist said that Sandra was with a client and would not be in tomorrow. Tried calling Emily, to see if Ray had stopped by yet for his haircut. She's out until 2:00 p.m. Tried calling home, to leave a message for Ray. The answering machine wouldn't even pick up!

Wow, do I feel alone!

I wonder how I'm really going to do it when he leaves. He's not the only one concerned about the stress this separation will put on our already shaky financial situation. I can't afford to live here without his help. Maybe I should take in a roommate, but I can't even begin to think who. It all feels so uncertain. What if he wants to come back? What do I do then? And there is the curious realization that I have never lived alone. I might like it. I went from living at home, the oldest of five, to being married. I've never had time in any space that was totally mine. How would that feel?

Right now, I just want to list everything that I will miss about Ray. I know I shouldn't do this but I want to get it out on paper so there are no surprises the first day he's officially gone.

Okay, here goes: I'll miss hearing his greeting on the answering machine. But then, I guess I won't have a reason to call home and I'll miss that too. So many times in the day I called just to hear his voice. I'll miss his surprising me at the train station, after dark, to drive me to my car. I'll miss the sense of security that comes with his knowing my schedule – tracking me if I am running late or don't show up. We have always kept such close tabs on each other. Now I won't know where he is. Being disconnected scares me. I'll miss our exploring. Making discoveries together. I'll miss browsing with him in odd little shops and thrift stores and yard sales. God – a man who loves to browse, not race through life! I'll miss the glassy twinkle in his eyes, with that cute little side grin thing he does. Waving good-bye every time one of us left the house – a silly little ritual. Even when we were mad and fighting, we never let the other go out into the world without that wave. Well, maybe a few times. But we both agreed it left us with an empty feeling. I'll miss helping him pick his wardrobe for an audition, but then I guess that is part of the caretaking he doesn't want. I wonder how I'll feel when I see him on TV. Now someone else will be sharing that with him. I'll miss the feel of his arms around me and my hand in his. Hearing him breathe when I wake in the night. The special blend of oils he wears. How he smells in bed beside me. Damn. I'll probably even miss the smell of cigars on him!

I'll miss our lovemaking – but then I've missed him that way for a long time now.

Actually, there have already been many times when I've missed him. When he's been right here but not present. Even so, this list reminds me that it has not been all bad. That we were attentive to each other.

I had the strength and resolve to do what I needed to do this morning, but now I feel absolutely deflated and incapable. Being without him scares me. Even though I came off as independent – emotionally, I always put him first. My independence was conditional on his being here.

A song is playing on the radio in the showroom across the hall. It speaks of love and lies. I swear, I've heard it five times today already. Once even as background music when I was on hold, waiting for my friend Natalie to pick-up. Is God trying to tell me something, or is the universe playing a morose game with me?

In a strange way, I am starting to feel better. Like I've purged.

JOURNAL • Saturday Morning, March 12

Sitting here in Ray's office with the faint smell of cigars lingering in the air. So much is going through my head. Last night I felt relief when he said he didn't discount the possibility that we may find ourselves together again. I don't recall the exact words. I only know that he had not said them before. Even hearing this does not make it easier. The doubts come barreling in.

This said to you by a man confused. How can you place any more hope or stock in what he said to you last night, than in what he didn't say the nights previous?

I reminded him that the first words out of his mouth, the night he expressed his desire for a separation, had to do with another woman. How could I not assume that she was the sole reason for his leaving – even though he gave me others. He admitted that was, in part, what he believed at the time but that, in talking yesterday with Cliff, Natalie's husband, he'd become aware of a shift in his thinking. Now he knows he has to be on his own to do what he needs to do. Period. Yet he still wants to see her. And that still frightens me.

God, I am letting go of her because that is where my ego will hang me. I will trust You with the details of how all this is to happen. Keep pushing me through. I don't want my fear to slow this process down.

THE FLOWERS • JOURNAL
Sunday, 1:15 a.m., March 13

Again, I write in the hope that I can put these words on paper so I can go back to bed and sleep – without the aid of sleeping pills. The events of late yesterday morning are racing through my mind. Ray and I were having such a good talk. There was a feeling of hope. Then bam! How something can get out of hand so fast! I feel so bad about what happened. About Peggy trying to calm us down and Ray yelling at her. No one in my family has ever heard him raise his voice or even seen him angry. I know this is no easier for her than for me. She has the complication of trying to protect me, while grieving for the Ray she has lost as well. He is as much a stranger to her as he is to me. What a mess. I hope he decides to stay at his Mom's until Peg leaves.

Damn. Why couldn't he have just lied? How could I have known about the flowers he sent her? It came through like a bolt of lightning. A lousy time to be telepathic! Why did I even ask him?

Tonight, when Peg and I were at the Italian restaurant with Cliff and Natalie, I kept wondering what I would do if I saw them walk in – wondering what part of town she lives in – wondering if a romantic dinner went with those damn flowers!

I cannot live like this. I can't be the only one responsible for the failure of this relationship – but I can't get clear on what I think was my part in it. Everything feels upside down.

He has to move out and I have to be firm in that. I've already lost him. Getting him out of the house just makes it official and will start getting me through those "firsts" without him. That's why I had to know about the flowers. Why you guys had to tell me. I needed to see. And I need to remember this is not Ray. He is possessed by something too bizarre for me to deal with. He is yours. All yours. Now, help me sleep. Thank you.

JOURNAL • Monday, 4:30 a.m., March 14

That perverted, twisted little voice in me that I call ego, will not rest. It tells me that she has something I no longer have. That I may *never* have had his love. That these past eighteen years have been a washout. A waste. A lie.

Help me get through these panic attacks. I feel I could just die, and want to, when they hit. Protect me from myself. I want this pain to go away. God, You are all I can trust. I have to remove what I've invested in Ray. Every hope. Every expectation. Every guilt. Every regret. Every reference I've used to measure the value of our marriage. Of myself as a woman – as a wife. I give it all to You, once again, for safekeeping and my sanity. Thank You.

And thank You for Peggy. She's been a real trooper. Ray didn't come back last night. I don't know if he stayed with his Mom or with *her*. But why should it matter at this point? I felt so anxious most of the day. I just wanted to crawl out of my skin. Peg got some boxes from the liquor store and we started packing up Ray's elephant collection. She said I needed to do it as a symbolic act of releasing Ray, and this collection was the most representative of him right now. Heavy! It took four boxes to do it. We hauled them right up to the attic.

I know she's afraid that I'm going to back down and let him stay here. She keeps reminding me – this is not the Ray we know and love.

And I know she worries about my not eating. God, I want to eat. I just can't swallow. I guess that's pretty symbolic too. I can't swallow another damn thing. I have no feelings I want to feed. It's as if I am trying to starve them out of me.

This afternoon I'll take her to the airport. Hope I haven't made a mistake in planning to take off the rest of the week. I hate to see her leave. This is a strange twist in our relationship. No more "big sister, little sister." I think we've needed to make this shift. It's just a shame it had to be this way.

JOURNAL • Tuesday, 2:23 a.m., March 15

Just woke up from a dream about Ray. Left me with a strange feeling. I was trying to win his heart back. Can't remember if I did.

This evening was tough, reducing our relationship to splitting bills. Yours versus mine stuff. I felt strong and firm when I got home from taking Peggy to the airport – but somehow it all got twisted around and I found myself feeling mortified and devastated once again. All I could see was a control monster called Bernadette. This is all he looks at to justify his loss of love for me. All he can see is the old, dysfunctional me. I feel helpless and like an ass. There never was any hope for recognition of my growth. For the things I did do right. We talked. I apologized, over and over. Sick for how far I had pushed him. As if he had done no wrong! God, I wasn't happy either. So why did my feelings for Ray not get destroyed?

I cried. He held me. Maybe he understood or maybe he was just placating me. He ran out of cigars so he excused himself to go to the store. Said he would be right back. Two hours later he returns, surprised to see me awake and sitting on the couch. He was angry because he thought I had been timing him. All I could do was look at him in disbelief.

Really, it hadn't started that way. Mom called to see how I was doing. Peggy had filled her in. When we hung up it was obvious that his "be right back" did not match mine, and the cigars were only an excuse to get out of the house. It was late. I was tired. I went to bed. I didn't want to be awake when he walked back in the door – but, dammit, I just couldn't sleep. I got up and started listening to old albums. Songs we used to share.

Why can't he understand how it feels when he calls her, sees her, and sends her flowers right under my nose? Should I be grateful that he didn't call her from the house? My nose is being rubbed in it but good. Logic says it takes two. That it was not all my fault. That he chose to see and react in certain ways. That *he* allowed it to go too far. But right now, it feels like it's all my fault. How do I live with this? Knowing his feelings for me are dead? I hear his breathing in the back room. I want to crawl into bed with him and wake up to find that this was only a very bad dream.

JOURNAL • Tuesday Afternoon

Here I am, again at Lea's soaking up some peace. Stopped by for the afternoon, after my appointment with Sandra. Ray is home – packing up eighteen years. I'm letting him take most of it with him. Most of it was his anyway. Family heirlooms and stuff. Not rightfully mine and, besides, too painful a reminder of him and a relationship that failed. I feel like I need to start as new and as fresh as I can. I know the place will be empty for a while because I won't have the money to replace anything, but that's okay. I need to sit with the emptiness and take time to reflect on what I really want and need in my life. I know I'll be fine, once I adjust to Ray's absence. It will be curious to see what comes in to fill the void.

I am feeling peaceful at the moment – or maybe I'm numb. Don't really care which it is. It's just nice not to feel pain.

Where is all this going? I want to believe that God joined us and that God will keep us together. I guess marriage of the spirit is something I need to believe in. I want a lasting relationship. But then, a hateful relationship could just as easily qualify as a lasting one. Perhaps I should be more specific.

This will not be a loss forever. For now, I will focus on what I want my new life to be.

God, please don't let go of me.

JOURNAL • Wednesday, 9:17 p.m., March 16

Back at Lea's. I had to take a breather. Just called the house. Ray must be at acting class. Maybe I should have tried to stick it out at home with him but, shit, he couldn't even pretend that it was hard to leave! Is he punishing me? How much he must hate me! Last night was a horror. In bed with a stranger. The anger I felt from him. If I am so intolerable, why didn't he just go sleep in the other room? I wonder, what does the house feel like to him now?

I can't stand this! Why can't I just believe August thirteenth's writing, when Spirit said I was not to leave him – that he would not renege? Please help!

JOURNAL • Friday Morning, March 18

Last night I tore up the copy of *The Artist's Way* that Ray gave me. Page by page. I was so methodical. So angry. It was almost scary. I didn't know the woman who could do this. I couldn't control her. Scribbled "commentaries," in crayon, on the pages. Things I have been wanting to say to him but haven't. I shredded the silk I bought on one of my recent artist days. I was going to make pillows. God, that hurt. The fabric was so gorgeous. But I couldn't stop. The paint by number kit I'd started, another artist date inspiration, was next. I loved those as a kid. Just tossed it into the garbage!

I am not letting him have any part of my artist self. I am accepting no contributions from him.

I packed up all our special love trinkets. The cards. The handmade gifts. The teddy bear that says "Hug Me." The black and white pictures from our honeymoon, when we climbed into that old photo booth. Even my first wedding band. (Could not pack the one he had designed for me, on our first anniversary, though.) Tossed *The Artist's Way* pages on top. A pretty dramatic statement. He can take it all with him.

When he got home, it upset him to see what I had done. He seemed really sad that I would have destroyed things that were important to me. Like they were sacred somehow. More sacred than this marriage he's leaving? He tried to rescue the paint kit out of the trash can but I wouldn't let him. This man baffles me. Why should he care? It was my stuff.

MOVING DAY • SESSION REFLECTIONS
Friday Afternoon, March 18

Went to Sandra's first thing this morning for a "Help!" session because Ray moves out tonight. I can only guess that he must have too because I saw his car pass on the highway. She never leaks anything to either of us about the other. As curious as I might be about what goes on in their sessions, I am grateful for her ability to maintain her objectivity and willingness to see us as separate people. I would really be hung out right now if I had to start over with someone else.

I told her what I had done, last night. She wants me to look at why I would choose to destroy things that are meaningful to me. She's given me my first official writing assignment, outside of my usual journaling, and wants me to start right away. If it helps to clear out this pain, I am all for it!

I'm to get a notebook and write, in big block letters, on

the cover, "Forgiveness Booklet to Purge My Anger Toward Ray and Myself." On the first page, I'm to write God a letter, asking Him to bless the booklet, take the words written into His care and transform them into forgiveness and peace. She says to trust God with my anger toward the things written and know that He will heal all. Then I'm to close with "Thank You."

Every time I am angry about anything regarding this separation or our past with each other, I'm to write in the notebook, "I am angry that . . ." and when I'm done venting, "I need to learn to forgive that." Then answer the questions, "What am I afraid of?" and "Why am I holding onto this?"

The notebook will come to sessions with me, so we can isolate and discuss its contents. Placing my anger in this book under God's care and resolving it with Sandra will protect me from the negative ramifications of needing to act it out. I don't need this anger to "recreate" my already screwed up life!

She wants me to take a second notebook and write "This Booklet Contains My Gratitude and Forgiveness List, Manifesting in a Relationship with Ray or Better. I intend to hold onto gratitude for these things with Ray." She says I will best forgive by offering gratitude. Not to throw the baby out with the bath water. What I am grateful for will become the foundation for a new and better relationship with myself – and anyone else I draw into my life.

I'll do this with the same spirit that I've written my morning pages this past year. So often, I experience writing as the only time I can really feel some peace. A lifeline in those long, lonely hours. I really believe it's the writing that opened me to this shift. If it got me in, it will get me out. I can hardly balk, now, at a little more. It's saving my life.

HOLD MY HAND • JOURNAL
Sunday Evening, March 20

Well, Friday night, Ray moved out. Inside I was racing,

but the session I'd had with Sandra helped to keep me acting relatively calm. It was so weird. He came in with empty boxes and groceries for dinner. He thought we'd have a bite together. Talking about this and that. Packing a box here and there. Like a kid leaving home, not a husband leaving a marriage. I was going crazy inside. After a couple hours of this, I finally commented on it. Don't remember what I said, only that it was pretty pointed and pissed him off. He wasted no time after that. It must have been after ten o'clock when he got the last box out and headed over to Charles's.

What a strange twist of inspiration that was! Me – of all people – coming up with a place that Ray could live and it working out. I don't even know what made me think of Charles. I just remember Ray mentioning him, in passing, as an acting buddy who rented a house down the street from Cliff and Natalie. Who knows. Maybe I was just desperate to get him out of here – or maybe I was desperate that he not move in with *her* – Shelly. Silly that I don't just write her name, now that I know it.

After he pulled out, my friend Angie came over to spend the night. I didn't trust myself to be alone. Saturday morning, she helped me pick up some groceries. I haven't been able to set foot in a grocery store by myself without feeling panic. Besides having no interest in eating, grocery shopping reminds me of how much I did for "us." Even with Angie, I wanted to run out screaming. She managed to keep me in there long enough to get a few basics and some frozen entrees. Smart. She knew if it took preparation, I wouldn't be eating.

After she left Saturday afternoon, I found myself sitting on the bed, playing with the wedding band that Ray had designed for me and staring at the cross on the wall that had once decorated the top of our wedding cake. I had this urge to bless them and was glad that I hadn't thrown them into the box to go with Ray. Thought I would take the cross off the wall and pack it away, but couldn't. So I blessed it. I blessed them both. Don't really know why. I just did.

Started my period. Hell, with all this going on, I didn't even notice I was PMS-ing. One thing about me, never missed a period due to stress!

Changing of the guard came with my friend, Claire, sleeping over. She had the same dream *three* times last night! She dreamed that Ray had stolen into the house while we were sleeping, to tell her that he had a special gift for me and that she had to make sure I got it. Each time she woke up and went back to sleep, he was by her bed with the same message – adamant that she remember to give me his gift. This morning we went out and talked about the dream's significance over breakfast. A cheese omelet and three pancakes. The only meal I seem to want these days. My comfort food, I guess.

Lea picked me up after Claire left, and we went to an outlet store that she knew of. I bought a comforter and matching pillow shams. Pastel, swirling brush strokes of pinks and greens, with purple accents. I needed to make the bed look like my bed – not *our* bed. It's a start in an otherwise empty, echoing house.

I think I'm going to be spending a lot of time in here, on this bed, writing. The rest of the house feels foreign and scary to me. I can't stand to be anywhere but in this room, by the phone – or in the bathroom! I almost feel like the little girl who used to hide in her bedroom when Daddy came home drunk. Or who was afraid the boogie-man would get her. Actually, it's not that I'm afraid of drunks, or ghosts, or of being alone – it's more agoraphobic. The house feels way too big and out of control.

I would not have gotten through the weekend without the gals. But tomorrow's a work day and tonight I have to make it on my own.

FORGIVENESS & PURGING BOOKLET
Monday, March 21

It's 5:31 a.m., and today is the anniversary of our first date. I'm wide awake and angry – absolutely livid at what Ray said before moving out, when he mistook my request that he sleep with me as a desire to make love. I can't believe he could say that would be an emotional betrayal to Shelly. When I wanted to know if Shelly asked that he not sleep with me, he said that he never discussed our relationship with her.

What relationship? That son of a bitch! He's concerned about his loyalty to her? This is insane! Did he think of the emotional betrayal that I would feel? How about six years ago, when they first met and had their fling? Not using protection – and *then* not being tested for AIDS until a year *after* the affair was over? How could he do that? I am so pissed!

And the incident between us last July, when I grabbed him and passionately kissed him. He reacted with so much anger. I was shocked. Mortified. Sure – he covered quickly with an apology. Said I surprised him. Questioned my motives. He couldn't accept that I still felt passion for him. I let it go, but now I wonder how I could have been so stupid. Why did I let that slip by?

Now he decides to leave and express all this passion for another woman, crediting her with charismatic powers!

I need to learn to forgive that.
What am I afraid of? Why am I holding onto this?

I'm afraid that I am not worthy of love. That I don't deserve a loving, loyal, monogamous relationship. That my passion is not good enough. That I'm not enough woman to satisfy any man. That I'm mother material – not wife material – in a relationship.

Holy Spirit, please heal these fears.
I need to learn to forgive this.

FORGIVENESS & PURGING BOOKLET
Monday Afternoon

I can tell right now, this notebook is going to get one hell of a workout!

I am angry that Ray is giving up his full time commitment to acting. That when he decides to be responsible and look for steadier income, another woman is his motivation for doing so. That he would be willing to do for her what he would not do for me. I feel used. I have always supported whatever he wanted, however he wanted to do it – to the point of setting my own personal dreams aside. I really felt, after all his ventures, that he finally got honest with himself when he returned to the dream he had for acting. I was happy for him. For us. And what does he do? He cuts out and goes running to another woman! I'm mad as hell that someone else will get to share this with him!

He seems so cold. He talks about "making it right," paying his debts and clearing the tab. How dare he cheapen our relationship to no more than a slate he can wipe clean and then walk away! What about the emotional, the spiritual commitment? There were many times when I wanted to leave him, when I thought I couldn't support one more venture, but I never gave up on my belief in him – or us.

All those pieces of me that I set aside. How could I have possibly believed that a lasting relationship could be built on a foundation like that? I thought I was being supportive. I didn't want to be his mother. I wanted to be his wife! Now, not only am I not good enough, but I'm abhorrent enough for him to go running as fast as he can to another woman? Damn his perceptions. Damn his deceit. Damn his games. And damn me for being such a doormat!

I need to learn to forgive that.
What am I afraid of? Why am I holding onto this?

I'm afraid I really screwed up and am being punished by

his withdrawal. That this woman can give him something I can't. That what she *offers* has more value in his eyes than what I have *already given*. I'm holding onto this because I want another chance. I'm holding onto this because I want him to see me differently and value me. I am afraid I'm no more than a caretaker. Not the kind of woman a man would feel passion for – or honor and cherish.

He says things like, "You're a beautiful, talented woman." But his actions say, "For someone else, not me. You're not good enough for a second chance."

I am holding onto this because I want to correct my errors in his eyes. I want to know that I can do this right!

Holy Spirit, please heal these fears.

I need to learn to forgive this.

FORGIVENESS & PURGING BOOKLET
Monday, 10:40 p.m.

I'm angry that he bolted as soon as we got into counseling to really start working on our intimacy issues. That he would throw up this smoke screen in the form of another woman, believing it to be fate, destiny or some karmic attraction. I'm mad as hell that he is listening to his ego, running for that "special" relationship when he knows better. I am pissed that this is our first date anniversary and he's not here and doesn't care. I'm angry that he's asked for a separation but isn't willing to work on a reconciliation. That he's pursuing a relationship with her. That's not separation. That's divorce – but he won't say it! I feel like a nobody!

I need to learn to forgive that.
What am I afraid of? Why am I holding onto this?

I'm afraid I can't trust him or his integrity anymore. That I am victim to his not taking care of his own emotional and spiritual business. That I'm a nobody who doesn't count, to be cast off on a whim. Holy Spirit help me.

JOURNAL • Tuesday, 12:09 a.m., March 22

Dear God, I'd like to know peace and guidance through this time, so I can accept the gifts that are being given. I did the best I could with Ray. He did the best he could with me. We are both worthy of love. We are both forgiven.

MY GREATEST FEAR • SESSION REFLECTIONS
Tuesday Afternoon, March 22

A lot came out of my session with Sandra this morning.

I have to find a healthier way to address the feeling that I screwed up, and the belief that I'm not worthy of love. That's where my panic comes from – and my lack of patience with Ray's retreat from me. I see his actions as proof that I'm not worthy – and I have no resistance to the feelings that surface as a result. They tell me that I must *earn* love. That I'm not good enough to receive it just as I am. "Screwed up" also feeds into a belief that I can never truly redeem myself because I'm defective. I've malfunctioned in my expression of love – and because of that, *should* be punished. That's how I perceive Ray's treatment of me. He's punishing me for being flawed.

Sandra and I talked about how my sexual fantasies throughout the marriage supported this belief. If I believe sex is a way through which a couple expresses love, intimacy, sacredness, and worthiness – all the good stuff – but don't believe *I'm* good – What an eye opener! I can't help but project my unworthiness issues into my fantasies! Punishment, if that's what I believe I deserve, easily expresses through fantasy. All my unworthiness, defectiveness, hiding behind the mask of playful kinky. Mentally manipulating – stealing every bit of love possible, before being discovered. I didn't have to be good. I didn't have to be deserving. My own secret pleasures justified – earned – paid for by pain. As potent as those fantasies were, no wonder I wouldn't allow myself to play them out. I was out of control. They weren't play. They were real. Too real.

Answering to the fear – the belief that I deserved punishment – at all levels.

If I don't believe I deserve love, I'll lose no matter what.

Help me get this under control! I see where this pattern has been present in all my relationships with men. Why none could ever last. Punishment came through withdrawal and abandonment. Loss of interest in me. Emotionally unavailable men, drawn to me because of what I feared I deserved most. I knew no other way to be with men. How could I attract anything any different from what I believed in?

Even with Dad, punishment was always to withdraw or withhold something that was important to me. And as a kid, I never remember hearing him say he loved me. I felt I had to earn his approval – and worked hard to hide my flaws. He didn't mean for me to react that way. It was just the way I personalized the environment I grew up in. This pattern with men became my story and I have lived it to the hilt. It's ironic that it has taken my husband abandoning me for my father to openly express his love for me. I know Dad feels deeply. Heart to heart, we are a lot alike. It's taken me this long to see that, to finally allow myself to feel his love.

I remember wondering, the first time Ray and I made love, "Why is a great guy like this going out with me?" I felt like an impostor. My greatest fear? Being found out. Now I'm finally being punished, impostor that I am, and this "great guy" is correcting his error with another woman. It's amazing we lasted this long with my carrying this belief.

To a lesser degree, I even have this fear with women. It's hard for me to relax and accept all this love from my girlfriends right now. The only thing giving me permission to express my neediness is the justification that in years gone by I've made "deposits" in giving my time and love to them. My fear is that I will overdraw my accounts and they'll withdraw their love. Do I only receive their love because I earned it first? No! Why would I shortchange their abilities to offer unconditional love to support my fear?

I also see a connection here as to why I haven't been able to relax and trust my spirit guides. God's nameless messengers. I'm not worthy to know their identities and I feel I have to *earn* the privilege of their communications.

And that leads me to God – and the belief that I am not worthy of God's love. I seem to be acting out an authority issue here – with the men in my life – starting with God as the big authority figure whose love I have to earn, while trying to hide my less than perfect self. Ha! The sins of Eve. I screwed up and had to leave "The Garden." My punishment is that I can never have that second chance to do it right and get back in. I am acting out my "fall" with God, through Ray. Which is why I feel so frantic with Ray. Somehow, I am seeing his rejection as God's rejection.

So here I sit, looking at this dark drama and how I continue to reinforce it – desperately wanting to stop. I need to diffuse this. I need to accept my value.

MORE SESSION REFLECTIONS
Tuesday Evening

Sandra had me dissect my negative core belief. It helped me get a closer look, without all the storyline around it.

Negative Core Belief: "I am not worthy of love."

This leads me to the supporting beliefs that:
1. I have to earn love, but . . .
2. I will screw up because I am defective, and then . . .
3. I will be punished for my defectiveness.

Sandra called the supporting beliefs "splinters" of the core belief.

While holding onto and never questioning or interrogating the primary belief, I display the following behaviors and attitudes:

- *Comparison* - To Shelly. I am lesser. She is better.
- *Aloofness* - Screw him anyway. Sour grapes. He was just a jerk in disguise.
- *Control* - I have to maneuver people and events to keep situations from going out of control, so he will not discover the impostor that I am. To the extreme, I have to appear more together than he – even at the expense of his self-esteem.
- *Anorexia* - I'm unworthy. I will punish me first, so maybe he won't.
- *Suicidal* - My life has no value because I'm not worthy of love. I can't go on living. I'll starve to death. Tie in to anorexic behavior.
- *Impatience* - I want to get this over with now, because I know he doesn't love me anyway.
- *Panic Attacks* - My God, it's true. I'm not worthy of love. It's the end of the world.

SPIRIT DIALOG • Wednesday, March 23

So, if this separation is a correction, why do I have to go through it afraid? Where does the fear come in? When I judge it as bad? Maybe the better question is, *why* does the fear come in? And what makes me think I can judge anything as good or bad? On what do I base that decision? I'm in pain therefore this must be bad? Is it really that simple? What if there were no such thing as bad? What if all bad stuff became opportunities for correction? Would it be wrong if I felt no fear? How does fear tie in with the punishment splinter of my negative core belief? I'm not worthy, therefore I must additionally *suffer* with fear – with anxiety and panic attacks?

Yes, this separation is painful. But in last night's *Course In Miracles* group we reflected on the distinction between pain and suffering. Suffering is optional. Is it not enough to be in pain? Why must I suffer? To validate this correction?

Only in the realm of punishment does the idea of suffering have value. Punishment comes with guilt. Correction comes with error. A bad tooth causes pain. Pulling that tooth also causes pain – but it is a correction, not a punishment. Suffering is not a requirement of the process to heal after pulling the tooth. Pretty silly when you think about it, and yet isn't that a belief I'm supporting when I choose to suffer through this separation?

Feel the pain, but with no fear, and the lesson will take but an instant. Behold the wonders of your Father who loves you very deeply and no longer wants to witness your punishment of self or brother. You do not have to stop loving Ray. You only have to get accustomed to not seeing him so often. Send him love, but send yourself love also. This is about loving yourself. How else can he see you anew? You have been so lost in him that there is no longer a distinction between your love and your fear.

Let yourself shine. Make the changes, fill your home with your energy, and he will see you as he never has. Do not be afraid to love him. When you are not clear on how to respond, don't. Just send him love and light.

Don't look for what cannot be given at this time. Don't ask for what cannot be given. Just give what you can and what is yours will come back to you. Be true to your feelings and keep your energy high so you may shine to him. Walk softly. Listen intently. And don't be afraid to look into his eyes. Yours will mesmerize his. He's not made much eye contact with you and so he has lost you. You need not look to the ground in shame. You are not being punished.

DREAM • Thursday Morning, March 24

We are at our old house in Oxford. Ray, his Mom, and I are getting into a car to go somewhere. I am in the back seat. Ray is the driver. The seat is hot from the sun, so I use a blanket to cover it. Mom forgets something and goes back into the house to get it. Jerry, from down the street, is clearing more pasture for his horses. It's a terrible mess with all the fallen timber. For some reason we comment that he's a fast "clearer." He walks over and starts to tell Ray about a place he needs to go. Mom gets back in the car. Ray is intently listening to Jerry. I look to the road we'll be traveling and see trees being bulldozed. I tell Ray to hurry before the road is blocked. I exaggerate the urgency. He steps on the gas. We drive onto an open road and up to a school building. It has many classrooms. As we enter, I awaken from the dream.

Hmm. I think I am "Mom" in the front seat as well.

JOURNAL • Thursday Afternoon

Dear God, please help me.

First off, it's much too quiet in this showroom. I have to find a new job. Something fun that will capture and hold my attention. Break me out of this rut that is so much a reminder of Ray and me. The part-time flight attendant position for that private airline sounds like it might have some potential. Emily's friend seems to like it. With its being a charter, I might get to meet some interesting people. Lay over in some interesting places. I don't want to give up Smitty, though. I'd have to limit myself to short trips where Angie or Natalie could check on him – or maybe I could find a roommate who's cat friendly.

I need to get more comfortable with being alone. I want my home to feel safe and cozy, embracing me when I walk through the front door. Not cold and empty, reminding me of Ray's absence. The bedroom is feeling better. I guess that's why I go straight to it. But the rest of the house – God, You gotta help me. My love for music and art is tangled up in memories of Ray. I want to let go of the self-imposed silence at home but so many songs leave me sad and reminiscent. And I'm afraid my artist's block will dig in even deeper. I need a comfort base to create from but I'm not sure what that would look like. I've tried to sit at my drawing board but the studio feels so isolated. Maybe I should take an art class. Break out of my artist's block in a group.

It's time to stop denying myself. Help me to see what is mine to appreciate. To make my own discoveries. To create an environment that supports and reflects this woman who is unfolding. I feel like I'm giving birth to myself.

I want to take advantage of this time alone to open up and develop a more conscious working relationship with my spirit guides and angels.

I want to be in a space where I can give Smitty more attention. He's my kitty now. I've been so distracted – and it's obvious he's feeling the split because he never lets me out of his sight. I'm grateful for his persistence.

And while we're at it, God, sleeping longer would be nice. Thank You for helping me with these.

COMPANY OF A STRANGER • IN THE MARGINS

Ray stopped by to pick up our old comforter. I was ready for him. Calm and composed. Glad I had treated myself to a tanning session. Think I might sign up for one of their monthly deals. I know it's probably not the best thing to do for my skin but right now it feels good to see some color looking back at me. Cover up these sleepless nights! He commented on my weight loss. Expressed concern about my eating. Not the thing I wanted him to notice.

FORGIVENESS & PURGING BOOKLET
Thursday Evening

I'm pissed and wondering how much effort Ray is going to invest in rekindling his "new" relationship. All the work in the beginning. The initial risk-taking. All this that he would not do for us, to reconcile. I know he's told her he loves her. Maybe he's even expressed the desire to marry her! Who is this man?

I'm pissed that, after having his love, I now only get his guilty concerns like, "Take care of yourself." Subtext? "So I won't feel bad." Or, "You can make a new life." Subtext? "Get away from mine."

God, not so many weeks ago I looked forward to our future. Now he's gone and I've got nothing!

I need to learn to forgive that.
What am I afraid of? Why am I holding onto this?

That I am not worth the effort, and so *we* are not worth the effort. That she is worth the effort. He sees her as better than I.

Holy Spirit, please heal these fears.

I need to learn to forgive this.

FORGIVENESS & PURGING BOOKLET
Friday, March 25

I'm angry that I now know what part of town she lives in because he let it slip to me when he picked up the comforter. I'm angry that I'm glad he's staying in this area and not moving down there – that I keep tying into some crazy hope that this means I'm still in the running. I'm angry because I have to work so hard to find a life for myself in all this. That I let his lack of feelings for me jerk me around. I'm angry that we only got to one couples session before all this happened. That I didn't go to counseling with him years ago when he'd asked me to. I'm angry that he's hiding in her now!

I need to learn to forgive that.
What am I afraid of? Why am I holding onto this?

I don't like the Ray that I'm seeing here. I'm afraid I might not want him back, and with that comes the sad realization that it is more comfortable for me to feel unloved and punished than to be put in the position of saying, "No, Ray, I don't love you anymore."

SPIRIT DIALOG • Saturday, March 26

Okay, I've gone back and read quite a few pages from my journal. I see a very unhappy woman in denial. How obsessed with Ray I've been! Even without Shelly, we could not have gone on without honestly addressing some issues.

I'm afraid to trust myself with the information you guys have given me. I keep wanting a time frame. How long before she's out of the picture? How long before we can begin to reconcile?

You have the period of a few months yet, with this emptiness in your home. The breakdown is already occurring with her, though he does not know it now. She is needed still, to make certain that you do not let him back in the door too soon. She is for you more than for him.

Can you not fill your time for even a few weeks? You will see the transition occur. Enjoy your friends. Use this solitude to know yourself and your connection with us. You must learn to trust and relax in the knowledge we give you. See, Smitty knows that we are here. You need to also. Even if it feels like pretend. Your imagination is so much closer to us than your intellect. You need not worry about inaccuracies. Your imaginings will be more correct as they come from your desire, your heart, and are so much wiser and "in tune" than your head.

You blessed the cross and ring because the choice was yours to make that intention, to know that you have the capacity to bless. It is not the Father alone who blesses, but you and the Father. Hold true to Ray and channel your sexual energy to us. There may be another man sent in as a companion if you really cannot "take it." This time is not meant for you to suffer, but to come to know joy. We will find someone who will understand companionship, but who will not be hurt when Ray returns. That decision is yet yours to make. We do not mean for you to be lonely, in the physical sense. Perhaps you could meet your tactile needs through therapeutic massage and clearing your energies. Try this first.

These are tedious details that can change as you do. The outcome is assured. How you get there is up to you, and how quickly, up to your ability to release. This is more on your part than Ray's. Your sense of acceleration is correct, but can only be for you.

He can be intimate when he knows his worth. Right now, he has nothing to be intimate with. She is a shell, as he is. A receptacle for his confusion. She is not bad but, once the passion has worn off, her interests will not hold his attentions. You have been hard for him with your ups and downs, but you do stimulate growth in him. She will be threatened by his need for the unusual path and will be frustrated by his pace, to which you have grown accustom.

Fill your treasure box. There will be plenty of time to show him your new self. Let the Bernadette in the journal of the past year come to rest. It is time for you to be, and to express differently, now that you are responsible for only yourself and Smitty!

Ray is responsible for himself. You can have him no other way.

Go in peace and know that we are with you. Tomorrow you will do just fine. We cannot say to read these pages to Ray until the time comes. Things are happening as we share. The picture is changing rapidly.

Love & Light.

SPIRIT DIALOG • Sunday, March 27

An awful afternoon, sorting through tax papers and receipts with Ray.

I can't believe I was so pathetic as to admit to him that I wanted to make love, one last time. And even more – I can't believe his response!

"Don't worry, you'll find somebody."

That's supposed to comfort me? What is this man thinking? I've already found somebody, buddy! And he happens to be you!

What am I to make of this? Help me out here. How do I know the words written yesterday were really yours and not just my ego playing games with me?

Only time passing, in your eyes, will bear the truth of yesterday's words. You still do not trust. You still do not let go. We told you, "Do not ask for what cannot be given," and yet you did. You asked for it and so have made it harder on yourself. Today has told you no more than yesterday. You continue to beat yourself up with looking to him. He does not know. His Higher Self does, as yours, but that is not to whom you direct the questions, and so you get ego-to-ego exchange. Let it go.

Wait a few weeks still. You think he will not be back, but he will. Tonight you saw how what he appeared to be was not enough for your heart and could fathom, if for but a moment, turning from him for reasons far more valid than his for turning from you. You see the break in your growth already. He sees only his lack of growth, but not in relation to you truly. He measures his progress in her eyes, not his, nor in relation to your union.

Put your wedding ring in the God box if you must. It really does not matter, nor will it alter the course. What will come to pass will do so. Keep writing. Keep playing. Sleep in peace.

Love & Light.

JOURNAL • **Monday Morning, March 28**

Dear Ray,

I don't know if I will give this letter to you or keep it to myself. I am trusting that I'll know what to do with it when I'm through.

When you left last night, there was an emptiness. Not like the emptiness I'd felt before, attached to grief and pain, but an emptiness with resolve. An empty *knowing* is the only way I can describe it. Not that I wish to take anything away from our past together or the love that we shared, but it was as if I saw my grief and pain attached to an illusion. Before, I grieved the man who left our relationship and me behind. But now I see a man lost – separated even from himself. How sad for me to see you so differently! A picture of a man I do not know. Your spirit has been absent from *us* for a long time. Sometimes, I find myself questioning the validity of your presence at all.

I'm not blaming you. I am not without fault and have spent many years being absent as well. But, in recent years, I feel I made some positive changes. I wonder if I would have done all that work, had I known what it would mean to our relationship. It seems the more I awakened, the more you withdrew. Or perhaps you just remained the same and grew uncomfortable with the challenge my growth was starting to present. I'm angry with you for backing out on what could have taken us to a new level in our relationship, on what could have allowed us to express a deeper level of honesty.

You say you're not substituting with her. Look again. You say you're striking out against your codependency issues. That if you don't stand on your own now, in this particular manner, you never will. You say you're in keeping with your priorities because you're not moving in with her. You're right. But maybe you need to look at what those priorities are. They're perfect for a man who wishes to maintain a safe distance from true intimacy. Your priorities are in keeping with your hiding, while they appear to be an expression of accepted responsibility. These romantic beginnings give you the illusion of intimacy, but it's a pseudo-intimacy. You don't want the real thing, and will shield yourself from it by maintaining this distance in miles and scheduled dates with her, all the while patting yourself on the back. With a roommate to hide your emptiness and distract you from yourself, who knows how long you could pull this off.

The sad thing is, *you know better*! And yet, you are using what you know to support this fantasy. I can hardly fathom what I'm seeing. Your words, though taken from your spiritual insights, are hollow, Ray. They have no heart in them. Only intellectual justifications. Where is the love in your decision? Love doesn't exclude. Look at how much you're excluding. How you have to cut yourself off from everything and everybody to carry this out. Look at the timing. It's all here to see.

You know, I wondered about all the cards, through the years, with words you so beautifully scripted. I can't understand how you could have given them to me, and then do this. I misunderstood their purpose. They were safe for you. A piece of paper between us that would stand as evidence when your actions did not. A wall for you. A bridge for me. When I started to cross that bridge, I was blind to the foundation. Now *she* can receive those little pieces of paper that say, "Look at me and how sensitive I am. Maintain the distance and I will stay with you forever." My only fault was that I dared to stop maintaining the distance. I took you at your words.

There was no problem between us that we could not have resolved. You think this decision of yours reflects courage? Courage would have been to stay. Picking the lesser of that which you fear is not courage. I still love you and see that you can do this no other way.

You're right about one thing. I will be fine. I see now that I'm not being punished, but protected. Not trampled, but lifted. I still hold hope for the day when your eyes open – but more than your eyes, your heart. I can't hold onto the hope that I'll be there when it happens. I'm not strong enough to hope for that and get on with my life without setting limits on what I think that life should be. I will know love. I will know peace. And I hold to the same for you.

Eternally, B.

FORGIVENESS & PURGING BOOKLET
Monday, March 28

It pisses me off that Ray is over there in his new place with a buddy to distract him during the week and a girlfriend on weekends – and I'm alone trying to face what's happening, with no place to hide. It is so unnatural being here, knowing that he's not coming home to me.

And tonight, dammit, I don't even have a working phone!

How could he so calmly say to me, "Someday you'll find somebody." Has he gone completely mad? God, I hope she dumps him. I hope he hurts!

I need to learn to forgive that.
What am I afraid of? Why am I holding onto this?

I'm afraid because I feel that I have no choice – no say in what happens to me. Just like with my phone. It's dead. Cut off with no warning. I feel powerless and panicked! I feel helpless and empty. I feel alone and in need of companionship – but I'm afraid of what's out there to meet me. I want Ray to come back.

SPIRIT DIALOG • Monday, 9:45 p.m.

Thanks for sending Angie over. The timing could not have been more perfect, as I'm sure you know. How can I come to feel you more clearly? I've heard how others sense their spirit guides coming in – and yet I don't seem to notice anything but a peace when I write your words.

Removing sugar from your diet has helped but you need to drink more water as a "conductor." Dance movements speak to you. The hand and arm motions give homage to your energy shifting. It is as ritual, and yet is effective for controlling the flow and adjustments to your vibration. Do so more often, and do not forget to "intend" as you do so. Notice physical sensations.

Your phone service is out to keep you still. To keep you from hiding in its distraction. We can better control the influx of impressions. You are much too tired tonight for more. Go and rest.

Love & Light.

SESSION REFLECTIONS • Tuesday, March 29

Where did my imaginings take me?

I was afraid Ray would find another woman because he no longer seemed to desire me.

How did I reinforce that fear?

I tried to make him jealous last July, during the show. I whined that he wasn't giving me enough attention. I carried on, in my morning pages, about "cutting him loose." I fancied having an affair, so I could have my sexual needs met.

Positive moves countering that fear before Ray left?

I talked with Natalie about my sexual frustrations, so she would remind me of my desire *not* to go outside the marriage to satisfy my needs. I wrote in my journal to counter complacency and denial. I tried to communicate with him about my concerns. I agreed to couples counseling with Sandra.

Positive moves now that Ray is gone?

Work on clearing myself – and my remorse. Visualize a new life with Ray. Imagine our reunion. See him giving me positive attention. See me accepting it. See forgiveness. Be patient. There is nothing to *do* for Ray's love. Cutting my hair, restyling my clothes and my home, can quickly turn into earning – manipulating – love, if done for him and not for me. Just *be* and allow the new energy coming through me to do what it will. At some level of awareness, he will feel the difference and it may give him freedom to return safely to a relationship with a woman being, not a woman doing.

I can imagine myself receiving tokens of love for no reason that *I have earned*! I can see myself being pampered, nourished. I can lovingly *emote* this. Emotion backing imagination. This is how I create.

Something will happen soon, to validate the change that is occurring. Instead of trying to force it out there, I will pull my energy in through *being* so I can assert change where all change truly begins – within me.

I'm aware of some fear creeping in, regarding this approach. Visualizing, in this way, and *being* feel precariously close to a fantasy solution edging on psychotic!

MISDIRECTED INTENTION • SPIRIT DIALOG
Tuesday, 12:30 p.m.

Why my phone died Sunday, after Ray left. Why it did not get fixed until just before my appointment, today, with Sandra.

- I felt cut off from communication with Ray. Loss of phone service mirrored that?
- The need to cut off communication with Ray, at this time, is absolute. I have to stop looking for words that he can't give?
- My spirit guides and angels want me to turn more to them? To not use the phone and my support system only for distraction?
- I feel cut off from God?

All of the above!

Ray cannot tell you what you need to hear. You do not need to lose hope, but you cannot find hope in external signs from him. It must come from your connection with what you "know," as when you first met. It cannot come from him at all.

See how your fears have created your part in this. Do the work that Sandra gives you, to get clear. Your attentions to Ray continue to muddy the water. As soon as you start to see and accept, you start to stir it up with your "But, he's . . ." Leave his timing up to his Higher Self.

You are no less because he thinks he wants you not. You have always looked to the men in your life to place your value. You must want you. You must value you. How else will you know what, in your experience, is worth the attention and so the "intention" that you give? It is intentions that create your life experience. Where would misdirected or misunderstood intentions place your life?

Where are you now? Do you like this place of misdirected intentions? Then start learning and stop looking at what you don't have, or you will create even more. Consider the gift of what it is you can see and use it. Do not hide it. This "Now" shows you that you cannot hide it.

Do not worry about Ray, dear. His tune will change soon enough. You keep looking to him and you will not have accomplished your part, in the desired for time span. You will delay or abort. So get to work and open up unconditionally.

Love & Light.

DREAMS • Tuesday, 6:00 p.m.

Two dreams from Monday night.

#1. Ray and I were getting ready to go somewhere. I wandered ahead on a path that led me between two mountains covered with snow and ice. I had to clear the path, to pass through. After a short distance, I started scaling the side of one of the mountains to get a better view of what was ahead. I could see a huge fountain in a snow covered valley below. Its water was not frozen. I cleared the rest of the way and went back to let Ray know, but found that we were not going together.

#2. I went to the mental health clinic for my appointment with Sandra. There were many distractions while I was in session. I felt desperate for help but was afraid that if I insisted on no interruptions, she would get mad at me and disapprove of my neediness. Ray had come with me and was in the lobby, waiting for his turn. I woke up.

Now this is weird, in that Sandra's youngest daughter is sick and I had the option of rescheduling today's session to another day or going to her home. I was desperate to see her so I went to her home. And her daughter *frequently interrupted*! I was so grateful to be there that it didn't bother me though, and Sandra didn't seem to disapprove of my neediness – as I had feared in the dream. Only thing missing was Ray.

BE STILL • SPIRIT DIALOG
Wednesday, 8:30 a.m., March 30

I can attract love by just being. When moved to *do*, I must ask myself what result I am hoping for in the doing. Especially in regard to Ray. With him, most all of my doing is still about trying to gain back his love – or, at the very least, demand his attention. (Negative attention is better than none?) My ego says only my doing will bring me love. My guides say to be *and see the miracles unfold.* When I am being, I am focusing

the beam through which love can travel. It is as a homing signal, clear and true, not dissipated here and there, only to confuse and lose that which would come to you. You have scattered your light so much that Ray cannot find you, and thus himself in you. You must slow down. This is why you are alone at this time. Because you will do the work to focus and contain your energies. This is your part. You must accept this. This is why you are expressing your female polarity. He is "doing" because he must explore his male. If you both "do," you will both be lost. You must "be."

Practice. Ask yourself, before you do anything in regard to Ray, "What is this for? Where is this coming from?" Get clear on the tools that Sandra directs you to and use them as you have never before. The most "doing" you should do, in regard to Ray, are the exercises given in fantasies. Have fun with it. Don't be afraid. Your hope is with us and your Higher Self, so you will not hurt because of this.

Be careful how you speak of Ray. Do not let your words discredit his spirit or he could become for you what you say, and you do not wish to see that really. So be it.

SPIRIT DIALOG • Thursday, 8:00 a.m., March 31

God this hurts! I am tired of waking up, after dreams about Ray, and hurting! I had set the alarm back to give myself the treat of some extra sleep. Not to wake up angry and sad. How am I to *be* with feelings like this? I want to do something. To call him and cuss him out for being so self-centered, so unconscious! And yet they tell me to leave him alone. That his tune will change. Dammit, he's married and he's married to me! He is part of a union! Our union!

Just be! Just be! Give him nothing off which he can gain a perception of you or make a judgment as to where you stand. You stand doing and he can relax in your familiarity because he knows you doing.

How am I to visualize these scenarios with Ray, with this kind of anger?

Do not connect Ray with the fantasies when you are feeling like this. The conflict is too great and fear can come into the picture. Easier to have the man who is nurturing you remain faceless. We will insert the appropriate image. It is not your concern who will be coming to nurture, just that someone will be coming. You may have to receive from other men before Ray is ready, but that will be a better contrast for you. Though we sense he will be offering you something in the near future. He is lost in his world, but feelings, concerns for you, are present in him, though displaced at times. Be careful not to view him as bad. Do not discredit the love he gave. It was enough for you at one time. You just grew too much for it to be enough for you now. That does not mean he has nothing of value for you.

Continue to focus on the nurturing and "being" when you want to "do." Every time you want to pick up the phone and tell him off and don't, in the name of "being," you are making tremendous strides.

Remember we spoke of intentions? This is good in that you "intend" to "be." Say it. Voice it. Feel it.

"My not calling Ray is my intention to be."

It will benefit you more greatly if you focus on what you would intend, rather than just not call! It allows us to make alterations on you that are necessary, because of your willingness. This is your struggle with Ray now, as you perceive he is not willing. At one level he is, but this is still part of the "setting up the scenario" in order for it to play out fully. He will be willing, once all comes into place. You still must give it time. Anger and fear bring in thoughts of divorce. Not resolve. Wait. Be patient. Be! Have fun! Go out with those who invite you to play.

> *See how your fears have created your part in this.*
> I need to learn to forgive that.
> What am I afraid of?
> Why am I holding onto this?

APRIL

ANOTHER MAN • DREAM • Friday, April 1

Eric and I are going out for dinner. I arrive at his place, a huge mansion. He's very wealthy. He gives me flowers. We talk about the separation and my feelings. He understands. As we're getting ready to leave, he presents me with a white silk kimono to wear to the restaurant. There is a hand-painted symbol on the front. Broad yet delicate brush strokes form a red circle, and deep blue strokes run vertically through the circle. Very oriental in character. Very soft. He had it custom made for me. He kisses me and starts to massage my heart. It feels odd but I don't resist. I know that he's being honorable in his intentions and is not trying to take advantage of my grief or loneliness for Ray. He's trying to give me what he feels I need because he wants to, not out of pity. I'm grateful for his attentions.

Before I went to sleep, last night, I did the fantasy exercise that Spirit told me to do – using a "faceless man" that sometimes became Ray. This dream may confirm that on a deeper level I am opening to the idea of receiving love while simply *being* because I felt no need to reciprocate Eric's gifts or loving gestures – only to be still and accept them. As one of my oldest male friends, Eric was a safe stand-in for Ray. Symbolizing a long term relationship with a man whose intentions I did not need to question.

DREAMS • Saturday, April 2

#1. Ray and I are sleeping on a mattress, on the floor in the back bedroom. We start to make love, even though he is leaving me the next day. It's intense. Very detailed – right down to actual physical sensations. It surprises me that he would want to do this. At some point, I awaken (in the dream) and realize I was dreaming that we were making love, and see him sleeping, in a fetal position, in the far corner of the room. I try to wake him, but he is in a deep sleep. Then I *really* wake up!

A dream within a dream. How curious!

#2. I'm at a laundromat with Lea, washing clothes. I have a box that holds AA chips. Lots of blue ones. They are Ray's. I'm angry that he's left them with me – for safekeeping? (More like they no longer interest him.) I think about how the long hours he is working at his new job cut him off from all his support systems.

#3. We're at the house on Serra where I lived as a teenager, but it belongs to Ray and me. He's moving out. The house feels huge and empty. I'm afraid to live in it alone because there is no door to protect me from the basement. The basement seems to hold scary things. I try to find something to block the opening. As I look around, I see there's an aquarium in the kitchen. A bird dives into it – a red bird. A cardinal? But it comes up out of the water like a baby duck. It starts flying around inside the house, looking for its mother. I catch it, and when I look down, I see it's turned into a small baby owl. I release it outside. It flies away, enters another house down the street, and gets trapped there.

DREAM • Sunday, April 3

Ray is moving his stuff out. I find razor blades scattered on our bed. Some with sharp edges pointing up. I show them to him. I tell him that they could hurt Smitty badly if he jumps on the bed. Ray is nonchalant and doesn't see the harm.

SPIRIT DIALOG • Sunday, 5:55 a.m.

If you are there, you better come through with some good stuff because all I can think about is calling Ray! I can't stand this waiting! I want her out of the picture! I want him to hurt the way I'm hurting! I can't fathom that he has no feelings for what he's doing. I need help. You need to be here!

Just start writing. Just start writing. We are here, but your pain blocks much of what we can say. You are not making us up. You are loved by us, and by some aspect of Ray. You can call him, but will that give you what you want? You do not want his confusion. You want his certainty, and that he cannot give you. Allow more time still. He will feel what it is he does. She will not be here much longer. You are not making up this writing! She must complete her part of the task to complete the lesson for him. He can be no good for you if there is any doubt. Do not question how this is to be played out. He will soon start to see the holes in his thinking. Now, lie back down and believe that Ray loves you, even if you must pretend. See him at the door with a single rose. Try to sleep.
Love & Light.

BRUNCH • IN THE MARGINS

Met Eric for brunch over by Lenox Mall. The first time I've seen him since Ray and I separated. There was no kimono or flowers, and he's not living in a mansion. Ha! I think he might have been a little surprised at my appearance. Said how good I looked, like maybe he was expecting to see the worst. Bless that tanning bed, and Emily's magic with scissors and a tube of color! I don't want to look like a woman who's been dumped or to come off as a victim. Guess I've accomplished that.

It was nice being with an old friend who understood, first hand what I was going through without feeling sorry for me. We had a lot to talk about. It hasn't been easy for him either, since his separation. We shared some of the more intimate details of our situations. Our mutual sense of loss. The intricate layering of emotions that we'd been sorting through.

I guess Ray has called him. I didn't want Eric to feel put in the middle or like he had to choose between us. I don't want any of our friends to feel that way. I think he understood that. I do respect that he and Ray are friends. I'm just grateful for some positive male attention that feels safe!

THE STAND-IN • JOURNAL
Monday Evening, April 4

The weirdest thing happened today. Lea and I went shopping so I could pick up some things for the house. We wound up at the new home store. We were hungry, so we stopped in their deli to get something to eat before going into the main store. While I was standing at the counter waiting for my food, this gal caught my eye. I felt drawn to her and, for some strange reason, the idea came into my head that she was Shelly. I started discretely checking her out. Like I was looking for imperfections, but I couldn't find any. She was pretty. Trim in an athletic sort of way, with clear, radiant skin. It was quite unnerving. As I sat down to eat with Lea, I confessed my "obsession." When we got up to leave, this gal did also. She directed a question about the store to me, making conversation. She was very pleasant and sweet. I thought, if this is Shelly, does she know who I am? I hadn't found any pictures of her when I went through Ray's stuff, so I was at a disadvantage. Real crazy thinking. I knew it couldn't be her but the thought stuck with me. Lea started teasing me as we wandered through the store, trying to lighten me up. It did get rather funny because wherever I went, there was this gal. Like a puppy that follows you home.

I think this gal, and the thought that took root, was a face-to-face orchestrated by my angels – an entertaining way to encourage me to see Shelly not as an enemy, but as a friend.

SPIRIT DIALOG • Tuesday, 5:55 a.m., April 5

Guys, you said, when this whole thing started, "Time is not." Well, it feels real from this vantage point – and *very long*. I know I'm pushing, but I've been looking at our past, and major life transitions always seemed to move swiftly for us. We set the precedent for swift when Ray and I met. Married in less than three months? And how many other shifts since then? Why not now, also?

My heart is sinking. I've seen some rather unsettling and disagreeable things about myself these past few weeks. So many places where I missed the mark. Am I to work on all this alone? I'm still married. Ray and I could be working together on these discoveries. It feels unnatural to see his energy going toward another woman, or even toward a bachelor's life. And yet, when I ask about filing for divorce, he says, "No!" Why not?

God, divorce! How can I even think in terms of life with any other man?

Hell, I need to learn to be in a relationship with myself! But I've never had problems with myself for company. I've liked my times alone. Maybe they were conditional on there being a partner in the perimeter. Okay, I got lost in the marriage, but not to the extreme – at least I don't think so. I didn't have to be with him *every* minute.

Hey, how about a little positive male distraction to help me pass the time? Sure, flip from a marriage that didn't work into a dating scene that sucks! Think! Do I have one single friend who likes to date?

Give me a sign. Show me what direction this is going in. April the twenty-first is not far off. You all know that's the day Ray asked me to marry him. I had kind of set that in my mind as a cut off – a date for some sort of transition to occur on which to base a decision regarding divorce. Guys, you don't have much time.

Doing the affirmations and visualizations has been difficult lately. The tools you've given me work, but the relief is short. I try to hang onto their effectiveness, but sometimes it feels I outgrow them too quickly. I'm running out of stuff to keep me busy. I can't keep up the pace of running here and there. Sleep is all I think about, and yet I can't sleep. I'm afraid if I stay home for too long I'll slip into depression and become immobile.

Sometimes I wonder if Ray isn't really coming back, and you're just not telling me because you think I can't handle it. But why would you do that? If that's my reality, I have to deal with it. Why put it off? Please, don't play games with me. Sometimes I flash that he will marry her. Then the anger comes up and I realize my waiting for him is conditional on my being given another chance. Is it possible to go through this and not have expectations?

You have only to wait. There is nothing that you could do in Ray's direction. Only in yours, as you are doing. Trust your tarot cards. Trust your Runes when you doubt your writing.* Again, only time passing will bear out the truth of these words. There are still things that would be more than you could face, now for certain. You have only hinted at their possibility. The marriage you fear, to Shelly, is not likely, unless all is lost to Ray. He would be giving up to do that. You create this as you go, so there is a small percentage of possibility that could happen. But in our estimation, so unlikely, it is not worth the focus of your energy.

More possible is that he will be back and you will turn him away, though now you think you won't. His return will bring a whole new set of fears to address between the two of you. Do you, will you, want to work that hard to break old patterns? You wish him to face what he is doing, as you are facing your part in this. Then wait. He cannot be comfortable for long in his self-deceptions, nor in the events, day to day, as he has set them up. You don't need

---

*Ralph Blum, *The Book of Runes* (New York, 1987, Oracle Books / St. Martin's Press) *us to tell you the results of a schedule such as his, with so little of the customary support system. The love and support you alone gave him was tremendous in its quiet way. You were solid. A rock to him. He cannot feel safe to use her in the same manner because her love has not stood the test of time. Her love will be reflective of the questions that challenge his own capacity for love. How long do you think their relationship can last with that kind of uncertainty, really?*

Rely on what you know in your heart. Trust what you know in your heart. Too much still travels from your head, from where your doubts come. Your heart knows. Learn to listen to your heart. Learn to interpret the feelings of your heart. Be patient awhile longer, and keep doing as you have been.

Have a good session with Sandra. Pray for her inspiration as you travel out there.

Love & Light, Child.

SABOTAGE • SESSION REFLECTIONS
Tuesday, April 5

Sandra wants me to look at how I was setting myself up to validate my unworthiness core, and not really seeking love, when I told Ray I wanted to make love. I knew what his response would be before I asked, so my asking only supported a hidden agenda that said, "See, Bernadette, you're not good enough." That's why I felt frantic at his answer. I was frantically seeking punishment, not love!

I also need to look at why, when Ray expresses concern over my weight loss or how I'm taking care of myself, I can't accept his concern as love. I see him as my husband, withholding love from me, and so I'm not willing to accept *any* expression of love from him. Is he only expressing guilt in the form of concern, or is it really his love that I'm denying? Is this part of a negative core that says if I am not worthy of all, I am not worthy of any? And what am I doing to us ultimately, by not accepting any love from him? Will that not eventually shut the door on his love for me growing once again? "Any or all" versus "All or nothing"? Where are my better chances?

Sandra says to look at this attitude as my way of discounting the possibility of a positive loving reality. If I practice finding ways to accept or at least acknowledge "any," my chances for "all" will improve. In essence, what I've been saying is, "You don't love me the way I want you to, so I value nothing that you would have to offer me." I need to claim responsibility for my part in this reality I'm experiencing. I need to own the thought "He doesn't love me anyway" rather than project ownership onto him. To recognize that this is my *thought* about what I view as reality, not reality. She says, whenever I find myself in fear, to interrogate the fear and affirm the possibility of love with these thoughts:

> *How do I know that?*
> *For all I know he could be coming from a place of love* when he offers me health insurance from his new job. Does this sound like an offer made by a man who sees himself separated at the core?
> *For all I know he could be coming from a place of love,* expressing genuine concern and dismay at my weight loss.
> *For all I know he could be coming from a place of love,* sincerely wanting me to stay healthy while he is working through this so there will be a *me* for him to come back to!

When I express my negative core stuff, the thoughts are mine, not his. When I project my beliefs on him, I am denying him his reality. I allow him to experience a positive loving reality by not interjecting my negative stuff into his space to be *crystallized* between us. Do I really want to claim that my stuff is his when it may not be? Do I really wish to create a reality that reinforces, "You don't love me anyway"? No!

God, I see this. Bless the work I'm doing and protect me while I'm "excavating." I do not want the feelings or fears that I unearth to keep recreating these situations while I learn this lesson. I'm a work in progress!

I think it's time to make some amends to Ray, but I really need to be mindful of my wording so as not to reinforce my negative core belief. Phrasing like "I was wrong" reflects old victim stuff. Instead, I'll try something like "I know I reacted defensively the other night when you asked if I were eating. I wanted to blame you for my anorexic tendencies resurfacing. I wasn't sure what to do with the feelings your question stirred up, except to shut you out. *For all I know*, you were expressing genuine concern and *my* stuff wouldn't let me accept that."

Sounds awkward – but something like that!

IN THE MARGINS

I made this amend to Ray, Wednesday night. It was my choice to take this action, to claim my issues and alter their power to create havoc in my life. I did it with the intention of anchoring positive, conscious growth. It felt good to own this. He was responsive. No games. No twisting my words. He accepted it in the spirit that it was given.

NEW MAP, OLD ROAD • SPIRIT DIALOG • April 5

I could not go any further with carrying around this belief of unworthiness – unconsciously creating its scenarios to be played out in my life. It's time to wake up and be conscious of what I've been doing. It's time to change the script. To look in my own mirror. This separation was probably the only thing that would have caught and *held* my attention so I would stop and look at this victim mentality I support.

Just because he's placed her between us doesn't mean I have to. When dealing with him, I can still think in terms of *our* relationship, *our* communication, *our* future! Together or not, we still have these things. She is not in that picture.

Only if you invite her, and you need not do that. Do not invite her in. Pull your energy in and focus on the union of Spirit that the two of you still share. It has not been severed unless you see it that way.

I want to beat myself up for the paranoia I felt in the health food store last January, when I knew Ray was trying to hide something from me. I remember seeing him, out of the corner of my eye, whispering something to the clerk. My first thought: He was making fun of me. My second: He was buying something that we couldn't afford or wouldn't use. That he was buying a gift for me never crossed my mind!

I could feel guilty about that but if I look more deeply, past the guilt, there's a valuable insight. I was "living in the past" with him, as I accuse him of doing with me right now. I trapped myself in a "present" past. God, it is so clear! I gave my power away to the past. In doing that, *I recreated the past I wanted to avoid*. What a loop! I could try to justify my reaction by saying that he seldom bought anything for me, especially objects in "little brown bags." That's true based only on a *selective* memory of past experiences. And, because I bore that as my *only truth*, I lost one powerfully present moment that I could have experienced differently. Like a child, innocent and excited. "A surprise for me? Will I like it?"

How different that present moment might have been, and how different this present moment might be, had I made another choice. It still can be, because now I am rewriting that past into a better present.

Every memory that causes me pain can be re-scripted in my visualizations by asking one simple question. "How would that have played out if I had chosen love?"

I no longer have to fear brown bags and can even

assume they might hold a surprise for me from someone who loves me. The correction is made and will soon reflect in my life. So be it.

When I look back at the angel art exhibition we attended, I see the same thing. My panic attack resulting from *living in the past* with angry adults. *Ray-Dad* was driving the car, while *little Bernadette* projected into a past with her father on a tirade. How would I rewrite that one? I could have accepted that Ray was not directing his anger at me, instead of giving his anger another direction to go in – which was toward my criticism of his driving and thus ultimately to me. I could have chosen that moment to do the trust exercise that Sandra had given us in our first couples session, rather than question his reaction to the driver that cut us off. Instead of insanely screaming at each other in the parking lot and pouting through the whole exhibition, we might have walked into the gallery feeling closer.

If I can accept that my power is in the present, I can rewrite these events in meditation as if they are *now*, and know the correction is made.

If memory is all I have of the past, and what I base my present choices on, why not give myself a different "memory" to choose from?

With all I've read about how to use visualization and affirmation, how to focus on the future I want, how to imagine it as now and extend gratitude as if it has already happened, it never occurred to me that I might be creating this future out of a past based in fear. I struggle in my efforts to create the future experiences I desire when I place so much more credence on my experiences in the past. When I am looking to the future, how can I trust that I am not really trying to prove a selective past?

I know that my memory of the past is not always accurate, making it no more "real" than a future I have yet to live! So if I recreate a past memory that allows me to forgive, to let go of guilt, to feel differently about myself, have I not improved my present choices – and so my future? How much more effective to bring future *and* past to the present in my visualizations. It's all happening right here, in this moment.

Rewrite the past to experience a more joyful present. **Without the expression of fear based in memory, the future can better take care of itself because it will evolve from a series of inspired present moments.**

I have already benefited from playing around with this insight. Last night, I accepted Ray's offer to pay for my health insurance through his new job. Past experience dictated that I not accept it because I could assume it was a guilt gift, intended to clean the slate between us. Or, not accept it simply because it was from him. "He hurt me, so there! I'll deny myself!" With a little willingness and a lot of help from my angels, I accepted it in gratitude as a present "present." It was not my place to judge the manner in which he gave, nor his ability to follow through financially to give it. I only needed to accept it *for* myself *from* him. That acceptance was my choice, anchored in a change in my belief system. I am worthy of love and will accept Ray's offer as a loving gesture.

My angels said he'd be giving me something soon. I wanted it to be something romantic, like a rose. But that would have been easy to accept. This gift made me work to change, to express a new me in the present – and gave him the same opportunity. He didn't have to tell me about the insurance. I would never have known. But he did. My present is already changing and so my future, *our* future, will be better because I no longer have to draw from a negative past.

I asked for the birthday money that he was going to give me when he got paid for the motorcycle show. I was going to drop it, partly, because the check didn't come until after we separated and because of concern for his current financial crunch – which would have been caretaking him. But, mostly, because he earned the money on one of those first weekends he'd spent rekindling the relationship with Shelly.

God, I remember feeling so lonely and sad that weekend. Changing the sheets on the bed and crying, for no apparent reason. Like someone had died. I was so angry when he called after the show and said he was going over to David's. Part of me knew something wasn't right, though I didn't know there was a "Shelly" at the time. Now that I do, I could refuse the money as a "he doesn't love me anymore, anyway" guilt gift. But I am choosing to accept it as he originally offered. A birthday gift. Pure and simple. I am worthy. It is not tainted. He's willing to give it, and I am willing to accept it in the spirit of his highest intentions. An act, symbolic of my changing core belief. He is capable of giving. I am capable of receiving.

Asking him to take the paperwork for our tax returns to the accountant was taking care of *us* by removing myself from the pattern of cleaning up after him. I could see how letting him be responsible, as he says he wants to be, lifted his guilt for waiting until the last minute to get his figures together. There was a lot of freedom in his assuming responsibility for the action and my assuming responsibility for my own feelings. No need to nurture any more victim resentment stuff. Another positive present in not repeating past negatives!

THE VISION • MEDITATION • Tuesday Afternoon

I just had the most incredible meditation. Was out for forty minutes! Want to get this down, while I'm still under its influence.

I was praying to feel some peace. Closing my eyes, I imagined myself sitting on the grassy bank of a pond nestled deep within a forest and was settling into the tranquillity of the place when three guides greeted me and told me to visualize scenes from my past, with Ray, that I would like to heal. So, I went to a few.

Suddenly, I saw the bouquet of flowers that he'd sent

anonymously to my workplace years ago. I remembered how he had chosen to keep it a secret and how, when the truth surfaced months later, his response was that he had wanted me to know I was loved just for *being* me, without being attached to any occasion, person, or role.

I flashed to the drive home after work that day and how crazy I was with not knowing who had sent them. When the car in front of me stopped to make a left hand turn, I had finally relaxed into its being okay to accept the flowers and decided that whoever gave them to me, gave them in love. At that moment, screeching tires and a glance in my rear view mirror revealed a cement truck rapidly closing in behind me. Sandwiched to the car in front of me, with no way or time to move out of its path, I thought I was dead. I remember how the truck miraculously flew around my car, just barely missing me, and seeing the driver's face in his side view mirror, mouthing the words "I'm sorry," as he came to a stop on the dirt shoulder. It struck me how it seemed to be at the precise moment I accepted the *intention of love* from those flowers, that the driver woke up to the fact that we were all stopped and going nowhere. I really believe those "flowers" saved my life.

Next, I found myself in a misty kind of place with two figures standing maybe ten feet in front of me. It soon became clear that I was looking at Ray and Shelly in an embrace. As they hugged, I tried to vaporize her out of his arms and out of my meditation, but she just came back and reached for my hand. I was not prepared for the tremendous outpouring of love I felt coming from her, nor the gratitude and love I felt *for* her. I was shocked. There was no stopping the exchange of feeling between us. She took my hand and joined it with Ray's. She hugged us both. I saw her gift. I knew it without a doubt. The emotion was overwhelming. I still feel it as I write this.

Then I saw Ray with a single red rose at our front door,

saying I love you. I saw him preparing dinner on our second date. I saw us as newlyweds, dressed in white. Both of us innocent and fresh. A veil lifted and I found myself back in the misty place with Shelly, just her and me. Again, the exchange of love overwhelms me. I know that she is my friend.

Another veil lifted, revealing the pond where I started. This time six guides greeted me. As they circled around me, I noticed physical pressure on my temple and behind my left eye, as well as across my back, in the shoulder region. Almost as if they were holding me up. I sensed an acceleration of vibration, pulsation – a whirlwind of energy. I felt bigger somehow. There was a sugary taste coming up from my throat and my eyelids were rapidly fluttering. I had difficulty coming out of the meditation. When I opened my eyes, I felt dissociated from my body. Far away from where I saw my hands.

Slowly I return. Even now. I feel calm and at peace. Thank you.

IN THE MARGINS • Tuesday Evening

Can hardly wait to tell Cliff and Natalie about the meditation when I go to tonight's Course study. I'm so glad they have it at their house. Really breaks up the week and keeps me on track. We've all been talking about doing more socializing as a group. Maybe throw some theme parties, go to some movies. I'm for anything that could be a healthy distraction. Better than sitting at home, missing Ray. Between Tuesday nights at their place and Sunday morning's Course group at Berkeley Lake, I might have a chance.

SPIRIT DIALOG • Wednesday, 8:20 p.m., April 6

Okay, guys, what did I just see? What is it I feel, in regard to the Ray who just left? There's a freedom and yet, at the same time, a sadness. Give me some insight.

What you saw was the little boy who is trying to become a man, but has chosen a very hard way to do it. He does not want success in this venture, truly. He has carefully selected this for failure, so he will not fail in his intent. We are speaking on two levels here, and of his Higher Self, with whom his lower self is out of touch, necessarily so. The failure will be to the lower and, in that, success for the Higher, as he has orchestrated this so his lower self will not run off.

You are in touch with us, as well as your Higher Self, because your learning is to come now, in the emptiness. You will have your foundation in place when he meets his fall. His learning will be in the aftermath, and it is critical that you be firm in your growth so you will not get in the way of what he has set himself up to learn. What you do not feel from him, or rather what you do feel, is the nature of the break between his two selves. That is the hollowness that you sense when you look at him. The Ray you know has evidenced both selves. But now, in order to carry this out, one must be cut off. What you see is the lower self in operation, not knowing the extent to which he is being set up for a fall. This Ray, you are right, you do not want.

Remember this night, and remember last night's meditation in conjunction. Go about your business. Accept any moneys he will give you. It's important, in your learning, that you accept or receive from him what he is willing and able to give. It is part of your process, and will assist him in learning to give.

Try to avoid thoughts or memories of past events, except in your guided meditations. They will only throw you off. Now you must believe that you will be okay in this between time, as if it were not a between time. You just need to know that this is quality time for you. Why should it be limbo when you have so much at your fingertips to create otherwise, if the outcome is assured and you do your given tasks? Go out to the playground and play. Stop comparing. Shelly does not even have the Ray you know. You are not sharing him, nor losing him to her. She has yet another. Go in peace and sleep well.

Love & Light.

JOURNAL • Thursday, 11:00 a.m., April 7

So many thoughts. Last night was strange – seeing Ray. He looked good, though a little disheveled. I did not feel drawn to him. There seemed to be nothing to be drawn to. He looked like Ray. He talked like Ray. But he didn't feel like Ray. I found it disconcerting – and yet I was gratefully aware that this stranger made it easy for me to watch him go.

I do not want this Ray. The Ray I first met and married, that's who I am grieving. That's the Ray I believe in. The Ray I know. I'm sorry that he's chosen such a hard way to grow, but I don't feel bad for this Ray. This man will bring back the Ray I know in Spirit. The Ray I will always love. I won't regret our past. I will rework it in every meditation, in every area presented to me.

I now have a way to let go of the Bernadette who grew too heavy to carry. Who I never could rise above. I can and I am! I am better than I ever knew I could be. I have not lost in all this. This is a crossroads. Ray will find his way back from this plotted detour and we will go on together as husband and wife. So be it!

DREAM • Friday, 7:30 a.m., April 8

Ray is sitting on a couch, in a living room. A woman is showing him all the things she bought from a health food store, to help him quit smoking. He's calm, open, and receptive to her. I'm sitting at the other end of the couch and sarcastically remark on how I could never get away with that. She's wife number two. I get up, go into another room and slam the door. Later in the dream, I hear he's getting married again. This will make wife number three! I decide that I will not attend the ceremony. I catch him bragging to some guys that, not only will I be attending, I will be performing a dance that he taught me! At this point, we're in some kind of army barracks. I tell him I have no intention of witnessing this marriage or performing any dance. I look hard at him and realize, this is not the face of Ray. I walk up to him and challenge him to hit me. He refuses, so I hit him. I pull at him, and start biting and punching and kicking. As we roll on the floor, I'm screaming, "You son of a bitch. I hate you." Then I wake up.

Good venting dream! Especially in light of the fact that, in our worst fights, we *never* got physical, let alone into name calling. Today, I should be pretty calm!

SESSION REFLECTIONS • Friday

I am now feeling guilty for wanting a specific outcome. For wanting Ray to return to the relationship. And for me, guilt always comes with fear of punishment. "Look out! God is the Boss!" I have usurped his authority with my desire and he will have to put me in my place. Fitting that I should use lower case in "his" and "he" because only a god of *my* creation would act in such a way!

I won't be punished for having this desire. It's normal to feel this. And I don't need to feel apologetic. In this world we have something called marriage and I happen to believe in it. It's natural for me to want to see our marriage continue, as I still see it as good, workable – retrievable. I may not have been happy all the time, but I see *my* contributions to the unhappiness. In that respect alone, it could be more happy for me, and Ray as well, for my changes might free him to make his own. It's natural to want to take my discoveries and apply them toward this relationship, rather than start over on another. That's not punishable! That's commendable.

There's an emptiness, but not a void. Can I be patient enough to allow this to run its corrective course? When these racing hormones kick in, the idea of finding comfort or distraction in another man is tempting. But then I think, I have never taken this kind of time just for me and I like what I'm discovering. Am I not worth my own attention?

Why get lost in a quick fix? Being alone is not all that bad!

I see freedom and power in the present. In rewriting the past. I want to share this process with Ray because I know he wants freedom as well. He's just going about finding it differently. We both want the same and, in that, we remain connected in Spirit.

God, grant me Your love and patience. How do You do it when we wander off? I guess You know we are never truly far from You. Even though we might think we've lost our way, You know that we will all awaken and find the path back home. Or perhaps we will find that we never left home. Is that how I am to view this journey with Ray? Recognize that he is not gone and not lost? He's having a dream and, when he awakens, he'll see that this woman was just an illusion? If I view our separation like this, I have two choices. To share this dream as *he* dreams it (which for me becomes a nightmare, spiraling me further into the abyss) or go about my business and use this dream we share to correct in me what needs correction.

Sometimes I walk a fine line with these healing insights – a line precariously close to where my ego says madness is born. Their focus requires an attentiveness to this separation that takes a lot of energy to maintain, but the effects are more positive than all the typical "it's your fault" resentment stuff. If, by some fluke, we do not reunite, I know the changes I'm making and the foundation being built will benefit me. I might be sad, but I will not lack.

So many major transitions in our life together have happened swiftly, this separation being no exception. I don't want to be the one who prolongs this. I don't support a belief that says correction has to take a long time. That's just an illusion we buy into here. Healing can happen in the snap of a finger.

It's springtime and spring is a good time to prune. Dead branches keep the blossoming sparse. Prune hard and let us grow full. As the leaves unfold and open to their new season, so shall we. Let the Holy Spirit show us a relationship healed and forgiven. This is my most earnest prayer.

WOMAN TO WOMAN • IN THE MARGINS

Ray's Mom invited me over for dinner. Woman to woman, we shared a common grief. I know it was hard for her when Ray's father left and then moved in next door with his girlfriend. All this in a small town, with no place to hide. I don't know how she did it.

She was adamant that I not lose myself in this, no matter what Ray did. Said that she would always love me like a daughter. I think she's been afraid his actions would put a strain on our relationship.

I was careful not to ask about Shelly, but Mom offered that he had dropped by with her one afternoon. Can't say it disappointed me to hear that she didn't like her. Or that she wouldn't take down our wedding pictures – though, after having removed all visual reminders of *us* in my own space, it was incredibly hard to be around the memories those photos jogged. I cried all the way home. I think next time we'll have dinner someplace else.

FORGIVENESS & PURGING BOOKLET
Friday Evening

Ray, you asshole! I can't believe I let you off the hook so easily while our sex life vanished! All the time, not wanting to pressure you. Afraid I would injure your male ego if I seemed needy. And God knows, I didn't want to be the cause of any more complications. Damn! How long? And off you run with another woman for whom you feel and express all this passion? Hell, no wonder! We were next to abstaining! Know what I'm really mad about? That I felt so undeserving that I let my needs go while trying to protect you. If I had pushed it, we might have had to deal with it. But no, I couldn't do that. And now I'm alone. And you're having sex with someone else!

I need to learn to forgive that.
What am I afraid of? Why am I holding onto this?

I'm afraid that my denial caused this break between us. If I had been more aware, or less fearful, I would have addressed my needs and that, in turn, could have allowed Ray to address his. I feel like I made the ground fertile for him to find his passion with her. I want another chance. I'm afraid it's too late.

SPIRIT DIALOG • Saturday, 3:30 a.m., April 9

Well, can't sleep again, so talk to me. You know, I'm curious to see how accurate you are. Or how accurate I am in picking up the information you give me. I'm open for whatever you want to say.

We know that it was hard for you to be at Irene's, but it meant much to her. You are now as much an anchor to her as Ray, and in many ways more stable. This way, you will have a peace with her that you have so desired. She can connect with you, as well as Ray, as she perceives herself on both sides of the fence. This mirrors to her own life.

Yes, there are many memories in the pictures surrounding. Be glad that she would keep them up. They hold for you her vision of your union. Ray does not notice, for his eyes must be turned inward. But they will not be so for long. He still connects with you. His phone call should show you how you draw him to you. He could have chosen to call Irene at any other time, and yet he selected the time that you were there. You know your connection. He despises it as dependency now, but he will come to recognize its value.

Leave him be. His not seeing Sandra will accelerate his state. He will have to lean more heavily on Shelly to pull this off. He can-

not help but seek the support, and better it be from there. No one can give him enough, to lighten him, until he gets honest. He had to leave, child.

Don't worry. The work you are doing will show itself soon. You have been diligent. Be pleased with yourself, as you are there for yourself as you would be for a dearest friend. Your future is assured and your present already improved, as you have seen and will share with Sandra. The way is being created as you write. We cannot tell you exact dates, as the picture changes from moment to moment. Seth speaks true. Follow his words. They are an important part of your remembering. Your life will indeed be different from this point forward.*

You worry that life will be boring without the struggle that was so familiar to you and Ray? Don't put on airs. You will not have arrived. You will only be markedly better.

The real work is not in the struggle, but in the careful observation of and accepted responsibility for your creations.

Right now, your energy plays a larger part in this than Ray's because he is neither aware of nor responsible for his creations, consciously. It is not a spell you cast, nor magic. It is like what you call intervention. Divine intervention is, in part, your own, as you are of the Divine. You choose to be aware of this now in the work that you do and so, in a way, are setting the pace, as he must keep up with your growth, as you choose to remain committed to your perceived union in this plane. He cannot be left in the dust, so to speak, because of your decision. His lack of decision cannot vie against your decision. In this way, you keep the pace.

When you work in the yard today, intend to draw in the benefit of the energies given in spring. It is no coincidence that you are clearing out the dead debris in the midst of the newest growth. Even amongst the dead is the gift of life. Fallen leaves act as compost for the growth of a forest. Consider all the wonderful compost you and Ray share!

---

[*]Jane Roberts, *The Nature of Personal Reality: A Seth Book* (Englewood Cliffs, NJ, 1974, Prentice-Hall, Inc.)

We have not focused on Shelly because she really is not a main player in this and has the least to say in how this goes. She will support your decision, as she does this at your request. The best way is being implemented now. Know that you are not at the mercy of circumstances. Soon you will know what you know. Now, try to get some more sleep.

Love & Light, Child.

I'm getting that he will not lean too heavily on her, in an obvious fashion. There will be a degree of holding back, in fear of appearing too dependent, and it will backfire on him. Walking on eggshells won't work. His doubts will come back, as he'll feel emotionally dependent on her whether he shows it or not. No stable ground for him!

BREAKING OUT • IN THE MARGINS

Introduced my friend Barbara to my currently favorite store for earrings and clothes. She couldn't believe the prices. We kept the dressing rooms busy. I found some great layered skirts for ten bucks. Shear floral prints over black silk. Very gypsy. Very flowing. Bought some black leggings that I'm going to cut off at the ankle to wear underneath. And then I thought I would gather the skirts at one side with some of my vintage pins to create an uneven hemline and flash a little leg. With the black leggings, the skirts wouldn't be inappropriate to wear to work. Maybe a bit heavy on the artsy side – but, hell, it's the gift mart! I'm tired of safe and conservative. I'm tired of plain neutral colors. It's time to get back to that young gal who used to dig through trunks to find vintage clothes she could wear to high school! The one who wore her grandmother's costume jewelry and her mother's '50s jackets and blouses! The one who wore black nail polish that smelled like cherry and pale pink lipstick as eye shadow because the cosmetic companies had not yet invented it!

We worked up an appetite, so our shopping spree ended at the Chinese restaurant next door.

Samantha has been after me to meet this guy she works with – when I'm ready. He's an accountant of some sort, with a big salary. Owns a house in Buckhead. Says he could fly me to Paris – for lunch! She's known him for a long time and keeps telling me how nice and *stable* he is. I know she means well and is probably afraid I will attract the right brained, financially challenged, artist-actor type again if left to my own devices! Says he just got out of a long term relationship also. He's never been married, though. And that makes me wonder a little.

JOURNAL • Sunday, April 10

Just came out of meditation with the question, "What is best for me?" I have always been afraid to put me first in any honest manner. For years I could insist on my way, bitchily. (A word I won't find in the dictionary.) But there's a difference between *my way*, based in fear and control, and *me first*, based in love and concern. Even now, I realize I am still not putting myself first or considering what may truly be best for me. So much of what I do is still within the context of the relationship. What I believe I need to do, or not do, to "keep the door open" and not jeopardize the relationship further.

Is it really in my best interest to continue to hope for Ray's return, and thus keep the ground fertile and tilled for that possibility? Is it in my best interest to be keeper of the field when my other half is out "fertilizing" another field? Am I undermining myself? How will I feel if, say in two months, he asks for a divorce? Is it better for me to cut the ties now? Am I best addressing my needs by maintaining hope, or am I best addressing my needs by giving up hope?

I don't like staying tied to the rejection, the abandonment, the anger. I placed so little value on what I gave. How could I expect him to place more than I? I see my denial. I admit to faulty decisions and actions. I want better but I don't know what I'd want to keep in this relationship. I'm just not sure what was real.

IN THE MARGINS

Got the information from Emily's friend and sent my resumé to the airline. Don't know if this is the right move to make, but at least it's a move. I'm tired of waiting! Tried to play with the pendulum, the way Lea showed me, to see if I could get more definitive answers to some of these questions. Not sure if I was doing it right. One minute it would say "yes" then another minute it would say "no" with the same question! Hell, I don't need a pendulum. I can do that just fine all by myself.

SPIRIT DIALOG • Monday, April 11

Ten more days to the day Ray asked me to marry him. What about my decision to ask for a divorce if I see no change in him by then? And what am I to make of the pendulum information I got?

The basis on which you make this decision is good practice for you, as you are correct in that you still put the relationship first. This is not bad, as the whole is important. However, this is part of your dynamics because its base is upon a feeling of unworthiness to come before the relationship, rather than love for the whole.

You have feared to love yourself, as you have set yourself up to earn your own love by doing and giving.

Make note of that point! This is why you have difficulty being.

Pushing for a decision by Ray would be an interesting exercise for you in affirming self worth and in considering what is best for you to get through this period, but it would not drastically alter the outcome. Be sure about your feeling that, by asking him, you will be beating him to the punch. You cannot come from "You don't love me anyway, so I'll push divorce on you before you do on me," as he won't be asking for divorce. He feels at high risk already in being on his own and fearing bankruptcy. She cannot buffer these feelings for him to the degree that he hoped. You must then consider what best suits your temperament and do so with an attitude of "being" you and not "doing" Ray.

The pendulum has within it a degree of accuracy, as an outline. You feel it more. The time frame may be off somewhat. Can you not see to trust the flow? We can all try to push this through by the date you want but you will have much work to do also. Get back to your positive visualizations then, and stop seeing defeat. Watch what you give power to or you will fall in line with Ray's abstractions and prolong this period. You hold the beam with your intentions. This is why your motives must be clear in taking care of yourself. You do deserve better treatment, but from yourself. A self that is not focusing on him!

We know you hurt, child. We know that, by the nature of where you are, you will hurt. There is no way to make this easy. You think that by taking this stand it will be easier, and perhaps for a while it will. But you will still hurt about him because you still love him; and, divorce will not change that even for a short while. If you have need, because you question the foundation of your marriage, you can always renew your vows. Divorce might be a lot of hassle, for such a little while. If your timing is off, he still will not be ready for counseling. He may feel tricked.

He will be over her soon enough.

We understand that you do not totally trust this information because it coincides with your desires. But consider that your desires coincide with a knowing, a beacon to your own truth, so you do not walk away in disgust. Your "being" leaves him with only his own feelings to deal with. Eventually, the quiet from you will affect his own level of discontent, as you will not give him vent. You are as strange and different to him as he is to you.

Perhaps you could contend "me first" and want what is best for you but try not to label it for a few days. Just grow in the practice but let us show you how that is to be, when the time comes.

Know that you can ask for a divorce, in the proper spirit, but allow that still may not be to your best interest.

Love & Light, Child.

JOURNAL • Tuesday, April 12

I am starting to trust the integrity displayed in the writings. I feel the love and humor in yesterday's pages. Even though I wanted to push for resolution by the twenty-first, to be given the go-ahead to ask for a divorce, that is not what I got. The more I read the writings, the more their love and wisdom comes through. Definitely something other than ego, communicating with me. Thank You.

DREAM • Tuesday

Again, a dream where Ray feels like a stranger. And again, in army barracks. We were driving from one post to another, to spend the night. This was some kind of secret experimental station. Shelly was there. Our neighbor Jerry was there. Ray was passing her off as his daughter. I asked him if he had told Jerry the whole truth. He said, "No." Kind of smirky. I punched his arm and sarcastically commented on how convenient his selection of truth was.

TRUST THIS • SPIRIT DIALOG • Tuesday

This is coming through very strong. I am being told, by Spirit, that Ray *had* to make that call to Shelly. That it was agreed upon by *both* of us. That it was the only way to create the rate of acceleration we needed to rapidly overcome the load we both carried, and to get on with what we came here for.

He will hit bottom, emotionally more than physically. He will not drink. He will feel totally alone after Shelly, and must, to sort out his beliefs, as you have had to sort out yours, feeling totally alone in the emptiness of your home.

Your fear is that this is a calculated risk, which is why you must do your part. Not just for you, but for him. He is counting on you to remember your part. His thrashing about before calling her that day was his fear that he might get lost in this.

He has to put his acting on hold. He could, you could, go no further. It would have been half of what you wanted to experience with each other.

Trust this! *You prayed together. You did this together. You cannot share this now, as Ray must remain blinded to accelerate the correction so you will secure the understanding you need up to this level. There has to be a degree of doubt to make you do the work. But there has to be a degree of "knowing" while it is occurring, as the knowing is part of your opening up. This is a lucid dream. What you do for yourself, you will do for Ray.*

You must feel the past, present, and future as simultaneous. Ask your future self, "Show me how I did it."

Do the work Sandra gives you. The crucifixion is not real.

The army dreams symbolize your issues with men, organizational structures of which you do not feel a part. Male stuff that excludes you.

JOURNAL • Wednesday, April 13

Guys, I really feel lonely for Ray. The Kenny Loggins' concert with Lea last night was great. I'm grateful for the free tickets from her neighbor, but it was hard seeing all the couples. Knowing that Ray and I share musical interests, I could not shake the fear that one day I might see *them* at a concert like that.

I know my anger comes from hurt, from feeling cut off. I am not angry because I hate him; I am angry because I hate these circumstances. You say to do the work Sandra gives me. I am. But how much more can I do alone? I know: probably plenty. "I am but" is just another way of saying I don't want to have to.

This hurts! I want to pull the covers over my head and hide until this agony is over. I guess there is no shortcut through these feelings. Even in knowing what you've told me, and wanting to believe, still a measure of doubt creeps in and throws me off. Boy, this is a tough world to be in the way we have set it up! Even as a kid I knew I wouldn't like it here.

SESSION REFLECTIONS • Wednesday

Sandra wants me to find a positive core belief.
God, do I have one?
If I did, it would have to do with love. But what do I believe or know about love? Can I believe in something I don't truly know?

I can say I believe in the goodness of people and see, in support of that belief, most treat me well. Even people whom others consider hard to get along with. That could mean I'm just a good people-pleaser, but I don't think that is where my experiences originate from. I don't generally look for the bad in people, so I don't often find it. Therefore, something in me must operate under a belief in their goodness, to some degree. So why, if I really believe people are essentially good, when I perceive Ray as withdrawing love from me, do I fear he will not act out of *his* goodness? And if he was such a strong connection to love for me, why do I anticipate only the worst from him?

It appears that both my negative and positive cores are being challenged by this separation. I say I believe in love. In love's ultimate goodness. If I really believe that, why am I so afraid now that Ray has left? When he was with me, I believed that love, our love, could overcome anything. But now I see his love as withdrawn and limited. Maybe if I could still see love in him, I wouldn't be so fearful.

God, I am placing *all love* outside myself! No wonder I'm afraid. Can I forgive myself for seeing love as fickle and unattainable? For identifying love only with a body?

The confirmation will be there when forgiveness is complete.

THE STEEL DOOR • IN THE MARGINS

Ray showed up tonight with money for the bills. I think I may have made a mistake by inviting him in. When he sat at the table, we started a strained "chat" about the separation. I asked him again about divorce. At some point, I noticed he was wearing a new ring. When I commented on it, he said it was from Shelly. A friendship ring.

What? Is he in high school? I couldn't believe that he would wear that in front of me. That he would not have thought to hide it in his pocket. God, I blew like a silent storm. I practically hissed at him to leave. It was all I could do to stay calm. When I closed the door behind him, I just sank to the floor. Next thing I knew, I had rolled over on my back, and was kicking the door as hard as I could. Good thing it's a steel door because I kicked the shit out of it until the bottom of my feet burned. When I got up I could hardly walk. Went to pull the blinds and saw Ray still parked in the driveway. He must have heard me. Don't know why he was hanging around. He pulled out when I turned off the lights.

SPIRIT DIALOG • Friday, April 15

Am I feeling numb, or at peace? Actually, a little guilty for pushing the divorce question on Ray last night. I know I forced him into making a judgment but I felt I needed to know where he *thought* he was. I guess I am still needing to monitor myself by him. Why do I keep holding on, when he's not? Am I so sick?

I wonder if you keep telling me he is coming back because you think I can't bear that he won't? This is where some outside validation would be helpful.

When you seek truth, why do you think you will find only lies?

It is the nature of where you are. Nothing but the actual event will be true enough. You can get lost in the signs and not do the work. You have been told. Believe that it is true. At the very least, you were told on August the thirteenth. Before you thought it was real. Before you cared enough to be frightened. Go back to that writing if you will not believe the rest.

Continue your visualizations. There is still much in your past to heal. You see enough of the old you that would want to be reborn into control. That was a little "old," last night. You know exactly where the old you stepped in, and where the combination of you and Ray invited it forward. You are still too close to your mutual parts played. You must go the rest of the way in this journey alone, toward starting new between you. Go about your day in peace. Amen.

JOURNAL • Saturday Morning, April 16

Ray's right. There is nothing in this marriage worth saving. What I grieve isn't even back there. This new Bernadette who is trying to emerge would not choose to be in a relationship with the Ray she sees today. What she sees in him is not in her best interest to share. She deserves to feel safe not judged, so she can grow in trust and come to know herself in surrender – and in vulnerability to a man in a relationship that nurtures.

Sandra says I am still doing "all or nothing." There must have been something of value in the marriage or it would not have endured almost eighteen years. She says I can't determine that this marriage is *not* worth saving anymore than I can determine it *is* worth saving. And certainly not based on Ray's words the other night! Maybe she's right.

Mom should be here soon. I'm so glad she's coming up. How odd. Just a few months back, I thought Ray and I would be in Florida this very weekend, celebrating Mom and Dad's fortieth anniversary – renewing our own vows with them and the rest of the family. Wow! Just goes to show how you never know. Here I am thinking our marriage is strong and how wonderful it would be to recommit in this way – and *BOOM!* It all blows apart.

I know this is hard for her. She loves Ray and won't condemn him. And I don't want her to. She will pray like hell – for *both* of us. I know that about her and am grateful for that capacity in her. She's coming to be with me and help me through this time, even though she's grieving and trying to work through her own hurt. Damn, this is tough.

I also know she saw a lot more going on between us and with him that concerned her than she ever gave voice to. She's careful with her words and keeps so much to herself about what she sees, but my heart can read between the lines – because I know hers so well. Sometimes intuition is a bitch for both of us.

She is such a source of strength for me. I'm really blessed by her presence as my Mom. We've been buddies through so much. Who'd have thought this too would be something we'd have to buddy up for.

MAKING A HOME • JOURNAL • Saturday Night

I can tell that Mom is on a mission. We stopped at a roadside vender on the way to dinner and she bought a rug for the living room. Deep pink, with shades of green. Looks nice with the gold love seats. Warms up the room.

Ate at the soup and salad place I like. Soup is my second favorite comfort food. How I loved making it in that huge pot she gave me! Nothing gourmet. Never a recipe. Just whatever I was in the mood to throw in, until the pot was full. And it took a lot to fill that pot! Maybe I can get back to doing that for myself.

JOURNAL • Monday, April 18

Mom is really helping me anchor in my little house. I think the emptiness struck her. Had it in her mind to buy a daybed for the back bedroom. Something comfortable for my company to sleep on, when they stay over. I know she's grateful for the support my girlfriends have given me. She's come to know so many of them through the years. And knowing they are here makes it easier for her not to worry so much about me or my choice to stay. She said Dad thought I should move to Florida to be near them. She had to remind him that this is my home and where my life has been.

We shopped around Sunday and found the daybed I liked. I've always wanted one. Seems cozy to me, especially with lots of pillows. Trying to put it together was comical, but we did it. We also picked up a couple of art posters and frames so I can start branching out into other areas of the house. I guess it was obvious I was living exclusively in the bedroom. Eating on the bed. Phone by the bed. All my writing stuff within reach of the bed. My safe place.

She found fabric that matched some throw pillows I'd bought with Lea a few weeks ago and made valances for the living room windows while I was at work today. Even bought special curtain rods for them. She had a certain style in mind, something special she wanted to do with them, but they didn't turn out the way she wanted. When I got home, she seemed frustrated and upset. I could tell that she had been crying but was trying to hide it. The look on her face shot straight to my heart. I knew it wasn't about the valances not turning out. It was the whole thing – my life, my marriage – and her wanting to make it all better, all right for me.

I saw her so fragile in that moment. It didn't matter to me what style the valances were. All that mattered was that she made them with so much love. And every time I see them I will remember that I am loved.

God, I'm so grateful. How odd to be in such pain and feel so much gratitude at the same time. I look around and see Mom encouraging me to come out in my home. Colors I like. Art I like. A daybed I like. Reflections of me.

She even baked the turkey I've had in the freezer since

Ray left. I just couldn't, and she knew it. We shared a turkey dinner then she wrapped and froze the leftovers into meal size portions for me. I know she worries about the anorexic behavior taking hold, but I really think I will come around okay with this. I am making careful, conscious choices to eat, and eat healthy. I like the weight loss. I guess that's what my old anorexic thinking would encourage, but I *was* a little overweight before. And even though I'm a little under now, I think I am wearing it well. Like I've only lost dead weight.

SPIRIT DIALOG • Tuesday, April 19

This anger is tiresome. I feel as if I am being consumed. Hurt from the rejection and seeming lack of feeling on his part lead me right into it. I don't know how to be or what to do. I want to hit him, make him see how much this hurts. How do I go on from here? I know I'm being tedious. If he's coming back, why can't I just accept the present moment and go about my business?

Ego tells me this is all going to blow up in my face. That he will live happily ever after, oblivious to the pain, oblivious to the running. Ego says *she* is the love of his life and I was only a mistake.

All is as it should be. Come, child. You know there are no mistakes. Only changes in script. But know that you write the changes, and always for your betterment.

Enjoy your new home. Express gratitude to your mother for the love she holds and what she does. She has sped up your process with her presence.

Your anger comes from fear. Work with the fears. You are not so sad now, as you are afraid. Afraid that you have no value because Ray is temporarily blind. Temporarily is the key word. Give it until June the fourteenth, at any rate. You will see and feel differently by then. You must know your value before Ray can.

This is about you valuing yourself, so you no longer have to play the role of the victim. You will be getting male attentions, but a little bit will go a long way for you. It always did before. Ha! Go and get ready for your day. Pray for Sandra.

Love & Light.

SESSION WORK • Tuesday

Why am I afraid that Ray will never come back?

- *My Attack.* How dare he want to spend time with Shelly and not with me! How dare he call her and not me! He must not have truly loved me. He does not know what true love is. He is just self-centered, selfish, self-absorbed, and immature. How can he leave me hanging and not make a decision about divorce?
- *My Fear.* He prefers her over me. He loves her over me. His silence means he doesn't love me at all and never did.
- *My Guilt.* I'm no fun. I lost my capacity for play. I lost my "little girl." I told her that she had to be an adult, or go away. Now I am guilty for being too much of an adult (mother) to him. I'm boring. In comparison to Shelly: I see her as being fun and carefree. I see him craving that in a woman.
- *Can I forgive myself for this?* I want to. Ha! Now I have to earn love by being fun. It's more of the "I'm not worthy" stuff. Just because I got too serious does not mean I'm not worthy of love. I can correct this now.

Why am I afraid that Ray will never come back?

- *My Attack.* How dare he shower her with flowers, romantic attention, sex when he has not given that to me without strings attached!

- **My Fear.** Similar to previous, except with sexual overtones. He prefers her sexually over me.
- **My Guilt.** I let myself go. I didn't worry about my appearance at home. I put on weight. I went for sensible, practical clothing when I would have preferred something more feminine, exotic, even bizarre. Being the frugal victim, I settled for T-shirts rather than silk nighties. I got lazy about pampering *myself* with perfumes, lotions, bubble baths, manicures. I expected him to pamper me but left him no clue that I even cared about these things anymore. In comparison to Shelly: I am sure that, in her being single, she's on the ball, has a sexual identity that is her own, *always* shaves her legs, is in perfect shape, and looks gorgeous without make-up. In letting myself go, I let myself down, and he lost interest.
- **Can I forgive myself for this?** I want to. Again, I can correct this now. I need to see that my guilt is also an attack on him, implying shallowness in that he could not love me with hairy legs. Back to the core of I am not worthy. In this case I did not make the mark, so he left me for another. *My core belief attacks us both.*

I guess I want to punish myself because I keep going back to the idea that Ray should give me a second chance to correct my behavior. Every time I link my forgiveness to his forgiving me, I obviously do not want to forgive myself. The "me versus her" comparisons beat *me* up. How do I forgive myself for my mistakes in this marriage when I insist on perceiving them as driving him away?

JOURNAL • Tuesday, 2:15 p.m.

I say I am angry with Ray for making the judgment that there is nothing here worth saving, and yet is not my anger acting as validation for that perception? How dare he or how dare I? If I did not already fear that it was true, that I was not worthy to come back to, then I probably would not react so violently. My anger is connected to *my* fear, not *his* judgment. All of my attack thoughts are based on this fear seeming true, and lock him into this perception. That is what he thought and said *that* day, and it was something I pushed him into saying. It means nothing, except to validate my fear. How much of that conversation was my stuff projected onto him? I will own what happened between us last Thursday night as my projection but not my truth! Just another example of investing my guilt in Ray.

JOURNAL • Thursday, 8:30 a.m., April 21

Mom pulled out this morning at 8:00. God, it was hard to see her go. I just stood out in the street and watched the van get smaller and smaller.

NINETEEN YEARS • JOURNAL • Thursday

Dear Ray,

Today is the day you asked me to marry you nineteen years ago. Who would have guessed I'd be here alone.

I am working harder than I have ever worked in my life to find the courage to honestly confront the issues and feelings this separation brought to the surface. I have never been in so much pain for so long.

I am still the woman you asked to marry. The woman who believed in you and your love. The woman who never gave up on you and your many ventures and changes. Who stayed by your side because I believed in us when I could not believe in you or me.

You might be able to pretend. You might be able to be selective with your feelings, shutting out the ones that no longer support your newly chosen lifestyle, but I can't.

I may have made mistakes but I made them within the

context of a marriage that I thought both of us honored and respected. I trusted you and I trusted our relationship. You know how many years it took for us to get to marriage counseling. Making that transition to "I'm scared as hell but we're worth the next step of intimacy" was no small feat for either of us. And you, in the midst, are mysteriously inspired to make a phone call? Believe what you will, Ray. You bailed out on us. What kind of man do you have to become to pull this off? Or have you always been this man and my denial would not let me see it?

Yes, I am angry now; but, with what I'm learning about me, I know I will *never* have to repeat this lesson again. You will not know me when this is over. And you can believe that!

JOURNAL • Friday Morning, April 22

Ray, Shelly is not the betrayal. Not now. Not even six years ago. The betrayal is that you saw me slipping away, and all you could do was stand in judgment and deem me hopeless. How is it you stopped believing in me? You were burying me alive with every mental thought of leaving me. And when I started to recognize that I, *we*, did need help, you were *still* looking for your escape. You left me for dead, to dig myself out. You knew me better than anyone else in the world. You saw me in my weakest, most fearful moments. A "me" I would not let anyone else see. I trusted you not to abuse me with that. I do not have one friend today who would judge me as hopeless and see leaving me as the solution.

This is where I feel betrayed. You withheld love, when love could have healed.

CONFIRMATION • IN THE MARGINS

Met Ray's Mom at the pancake house. It was good to see her. She was a bit flustered though. Seems Ray has had to borrow money from her. Made me feel uneasy about what he's been giving me. Apparently, with this new job, he does not have enough left over his draw between commission checks, to eat on – and he's gone through his back-up funds. I told her I was not demanding money from him and that she should not be lending him any. That I was only reminding him of his responsibilities regarding the money we borrowed on behalf of his business ventures. That she should leave that for us to work out. I know she's afraid for him. He's her son. Her only child. But I don't want her funding this separation.

She also said that things are not going so well between Ray and Shelly. That Shelly seems to be high maintenance. I wonder what he must be thinking.

JOURNAL • Saturday, April 23

I am still amazed at what Ray's Mom told me. I should be angry, this morning, but I'm not. I'm just flabbergasted. I don't know how to feel or what to believe about Shelly and the pins-and-needles personality that Mom described. I know it's second hand but it sounds like Ray is walking on eggshells with his new love. What he has chosen to jeopardize for *that* kind of relationship reflects to me that he holds no value for himself.

God, what a mirror! He is working so hard to *earn* his place in her life. That is what I did in his life! I can see where this is about my knowing, accepting, and honoring my *own* value – and not waiting for him to.

I don't know how far he will go with this fiasco, but I don't want to play anymore. It will truly take a miracle to unravel this one. My prayers are for both of us – and that he doesn't take a drink.

So, I guess something did happen by April the twenty-first. I found strength to stake my claim and give voice to my need for his assistance in paying off the business debts that are still on my credit. The day after, I get information that reveals the dynamics between Ray, the nature of his independence, and Shelly.

Is the breakdown already occurring as Spirit has said?

THE BLACK TRUCK • JOURNAL • Saturday, April 23

Something amazing just happened on the expressway! I was thinking about Ray and Shelly, and what Ray's Mom told me. I had the thought, "This is pure insanity." I think I may have even said it out loud when, at that precise moment, a black pick-up truck sped up from my left rear and cut right in front of me. I would have been angry as hell, at being cut off like that, except that my attention went right to the tailgate where the words "Pure Insanity" flashed back at me. "Pure" in pink and "Insanity" in yellow. Hard to miss on a black truck! And not a bumper sticker. But actually *painted* on the truck! (Pink for love – heart stuff. Yellow for clarity – head stuff. A paradoxical combination, given the words.) And if that wasn't enough, a song came on the radio about a couple celebrating their anniversary! The truck then dodged back out into the speed lane and disappeared shortly after.

Okay guys, you were putting in some overtime to pull that off! I'm not sure, but I think I can take it as a pretty profound "We're with you on this one." Thank you!

SPIRIT DIALOG • Sunday, April 24

I'm back from Angie's and tipsy on wine. I don't know if you can come through now but I thought maybe, with as relaxed as I feel, you might more easily. What happened this evening? What is going on with Ray's calling me?

My, my, aren't we cute tonight? You will be this way sober one day. Happy and giggly. Now pay attention to your writing or you will not be able to read this.

Ray did pick up on your projections. So did Paul from your Tuesday's Course group. You are not mistaken. Paul is strongly attracted to you. Your projections to him are strong but, really, they started with him and not with you. Slow the train down because he does deserve better than a rebounding Bernadette.

Ray will be angry with you but do not worry. In time he will see the folly of his decisions and will feel quite alone. Continue to visualize. Your sexual energy is very high and projects very well. This is a good exercise for you to see your creations.

You grieve, but you are coming to see the benefits to this new beginning. Today should have shown you that you will be just fine. Many will want to serve you in love as you graciously accept your worth in their gifts of time and assistance. You are "lightening." Use your sense of humor to help you through.

You liked our sign yesterday? It was a perfect opportunity to give you the validation that you seek. You recognize that this is pure insanity. You see that, though the outcome is assured, you are not so certain that you want what you thought you would want, even just a short month ago. It will take some convincing on Ray's part.

You will have lots of fun. Even in your mind, as tonight. Tonight was to show you your projections and how you are loved unconditionally. Even in being tipsy! You will access this aspect of yourself without the "benefit" of the alcohol. You will be amazed at the lightness you will feel. You are starting to feel it now, when you are not in fear. You are tired. Let us direct you in your dreams.

Sleep well, child. Love & Light.

JOURNAL • **Monday, April 25**

What a neat day yesterday was! The night before, Emily and I caught a movie. She slept over so we could go with Cliff and Natalie to Sunday's Course group at Berkeley Lake. We all had breakfast at the log cabin restaurant afterward. When I got back home, Angie's husband surprised me with a freshly cut lawn. Bless his heart! I'm so grateful. It had really gotten out of hand. Later, Cliff and Natalie came by and helped me with the other yard chores – emptying gutters and raking the last of the leaves.

I felt loved and cared for. After they left, I took a long hot shower and heated up some of the turkey and dressing dinner that Mom had frozen for me. I finished the evening drinking a glass of wine and listening to the jazz station while painting my toenails red. Got a happy buzz. It's been so long since I've had anything to drink. I never kept it in the house with Ray around. Never thought to. Maybe I was trying to protect him? At any rate, I felt as if I would really be all right, even if Ray didn't come back.

Decided to do some visualizations. A faceless man would not do this time, and I couldn't use Ray. I decided to use Paul's image, though I wished to project the feelings to Ray. I left it up to my Higher Self and Spirit to direct the projections where best. Very powerful emoting. The wine helped. Not a necessary tool but definitely a magnifier. And I didn't feel guilty, for a change. Just giddy and anticipatory.

About thirty minutes into this, Ray called! He wanted to come by to pick up last year's tax forms, as proof of income, for a car he wants to buy from the dealership he's working for. I felt, at some level, his call was in response to my projections. He suspected someone was with me. Said I sounded "different." I didn't try to convince him otherwise. Childish, yes, but just done in fun. I tried to put him off until Tuesday. He wasn't happy with that so I told him I was heading out but that I would leave them in the mailbox if he was coming over right away. Silly me, I didn't leave the right forms! Went down the block, to hide at Angie's, until he picked them up. I expected him to call later, angry at what I had done, but didn't really care because I was having too much fun. Like a kid pulling a prank.

DREAM • Wednesday, April 27

I was walking barefoot on a sidewalk covered with melting snow, wondering if I would catch cold or if I should put shoes on. I decided to stay barefoot. Then awakened.

What's with all these snow dreams?

PICK UP THE PHONE • JOURNAL • Wednesday

Woke up missing Ray and our relationship. Was tired of carrying the pain so I got quiet and meditated. Saw myself giving the *missing* over to Ray. His arms were outstretched, so I loaded them up with all of our photo albums and wedding slides. Thoughts wandered to our early courtship days of roses and painted hearts. Again, I stated my intentions and asked our guides and the Holy Spirit to direct my projections as they saw best. Casually threw in how it would be nice to get a phone call from Ray, confirming the connection, even though I knew the reason would have to be business and not a conscious "missing you" call. I felt I got through. About twenty minutes later, Ray called and asked about our joint business loan. I'd almost left early for my session with Sandra but something said to hang around.

Thanks, guys! Don't know what it will all come to mean, but it is an interesting exercise.

Ray seemed disturbed when I mentioned separating our auto policy, reasoning that it would be cheaper to keep it joint. I think removing myself from his policy means this separation is getting more official than he is ready for. Like he might be losing me faster than he had anticipated? Like I am becoming someone he doesn't know and cannot predict?

FORGIVENESS & PURGING BOOKLET
SPIRIT DIALOG • Thursday, April 28

It's this investment I have in Ray that is causing me pain. That is making me feel the pangs of loss. Ray could be any man. Any man could be Ray, without the investment.

What have I invested? I could say *time*. But have I really lost time, or gained insight? How about *trust*. Well, I may not trust Ray any longer, but my trust in God is definitely on the up, and He is not going anywhere. *Dreams*? Maybe certain shared dreams, but my capacity for dreaming is still within, and I am rediscovering dreams I had before Ray ever came into the picture. Dreams that, maybe, I was not to give up so easily because they didn't seem to fit the scheme of things. *Hope?* I have greater hope for *me*. Doesn't that count? So far I'm in the pluses – and only minus one man. These are positive investments that will always bear fruit. Maybe not on this particular tree. But hell! Look around, Bernadette. You're in an orchard!

It's my guilt investment that causes me pain. Creates these panic attacks. Big insight here. This separation is forcing me to see *how* I invest guilt. It happened when I gave Ray the "make me always feel good" responsibility. When I gave Ray the "you picked me therefore I must be special" responsibility. The "as long as you stay with me, please distract me from myself" responsibility. As long as he behaved by doing these things – and I am sure so much more that I have yet to discover – I didn't have to look at any of it. I did not have to acknowledge that I entered this relationship with one hell of a dowry of guilt. I gave him the gift of my guilt when I said "I do." He got the best from my "I have to earn love because I'm not good enough" bag of tricks. And because of that "I do," when he doesn't behave, like now, I get to hold *him* guilty. But if it is truly all *his* guilt, why am *I* in so much pain?

Pain tells me there is more to this picture. Pain tells me this is one investment for which I cannot afford to let him have the responsibility. I can use this pain to show me when and where I invest my guilt in Ray.

- *Pain.* Ray makes love to Shelly.
- *My reaction?* Anger. He is guilty for making love to her and not to me.
- *Guiltless response?* Big deal! He's screwed up. It hurts, but drop it. He's just acting like a fool.
- *But I can't drop it. Why?* Because I gave him my guilt.

His making love to Shelly, and not to me, acts as evidence of that guilt. I am guilty and don't deserve his lovemaking. That is what happens when I invest guilt in a relationship.

- *Pain.* Ray would rather sleep alone, live with a roommate he hardly knows, than stay with me and work this out.
- *My reaction?* Anger. He is guilty for turning his back on our marriage.
- *Guiltless response?* Big deal. He's screwed up and going through some changes. It hurts, but drop it. He's acting like a fool.
- *But I can't drop it. Why?* Because I gave him my guilt.

His leaving me acts as evidence of that guilt. I am guilty and don't deserve to be his wife. Everything he does, or does not do, becomes a judgment on me. That is what happens when I invest guilt in a "special" relationship.

You no longer need to invest your guilt in Ray. Pull your guilt away from Ray. Pull it out and see it as your own projection.
Find your fear, and so your guilt hiding behind it. *Own your guilt. Allow it to be a nameless guilt. Visualize placing it in front of you in a box, not in the form of a man, and say:*

"This is my guilt, unattached to any form,
and unattached to my form. It is here, in this box,
and I don't know what to do with it. Holy Spirit, please look at
this guilt with me and help me to not project it onto another.
Help me to know peace, as I try to extricate myself from the
effects of this special relationship with Ray. Amen."

This feels like a powerful meditation, guys. It seems rather weird, putting my guilt in a "box." Ego says that's dumb and won't do anything for me. I'm not sure if I will be able to catch myself in the act. I am guessing my pain will be a big clue, and trust that you will prompt me. Thank you.

Every memory that causes me pain can be re-scripted in my visualizations by asking one simple question. "How would that have played out if I had chosen love?"

MAY

SECOND GUESSING • SPIRIT DIALOG • Sunday, May 1

This is incredibly hard. Why can I not just relax with the information coming through my meditations and visualizations? Why do I still get caught up in wanting "specifics and signs" when I feel the what-ifs coming on? I am worn out!

Save this for morning. You are trying to force communication with us. You already have the tools you need, so work on those, and sleep well.

You fear that Ray will not be back and yet you must know that you have never parted in Spirit. What you do, you do for each other. Trust the Christ in him to pull this through. Last night's fear of his moving in with Shelly was an ego attack. You need not be concerned with that. All is as it should be. Sit tight another few weeks. Your meditations are assisting you both. Some of what you feel is not all yours. There is an aspect of him that is missing his connection with you. Can you not see how the purging in this separation will give you something you could have never had any other way? All you can do now is wait and see. Amen.

JOURNAL • Monday, May 2

Bolted up at 3:30 a.m. in absolute fear. Again, I could not get the idea out of my head that Ray is going to move in with Shelly. All kinds of scenarios flashing before me. Playing detective and following him – confronting her face to face – the two of them slipping out of state – eloping – never to be seen again.

I feel as if I'm under ego attack for putting my guilt in "the box." Not projecting it onto Ray has left me vulnerable to wanting him. It is much easier when I can make him the bad guy and just be angry.

I don't know from what direction ego is going to come next. Fear seems to be everywhere. Why can't I rest in the writings? Do I fear lying to myself, in the name of Spirit? Am I afraid that my call for love *will* be answered, as Natalie suggested? Is ego trying to throw me off? Misleading me with the belief that I am afraid Ray will not return, when in fact I'm afraid he *will* return? What if I don't have what it takes to be in a healthy relationship? What if I got comfortable with the sick little ruts, the nasty old patterns? Better to be distracted with the fear of losing him forever than to find out my call for love was just a bluff, just lip service to an ideal I cannot live up to. Better to let him be the obvious bad guy and keep my secret safe.

As I'm writing this, I am seeing the pure insanity of my own convoluted thinking. I can't figure this out and I'm crazy for even trying. I'm absolutely lost in the chatter in my own head. I don't know whose agenda I am following – in believing he will – in fearing he won't! I love him but I can't trust him. I can't even trust me. Where do I place my trust?

What is best to come of this? I've already stated my preference. "Dear Holy Spirit, Save me. Save Ray. Save the marriage!" That's it. Pure and simple. But then I go on to say *how* that should happen. "Don't let him move in with her – Let me know by June the fourteenth – blah, blah, blah."

Do you trust in the Holy Spirit, Bernadette? That's what this is about. Not do you trust Ray. Do you trust in the Holy Spirit? That is the only way you are going to get through this dream. That is what this attack is all about. That is how to remove yourself from the battleground. Trust the Holy Spirit. Make a decision to be willing to trust. Your ego is kicking up dust to keep you from seeing this.

Okay, so I can drive myself crazy trying to read between the lines. Or I can choose to trust the Holy Spirit and keep my sanity. Is that such a hard decision?

IN THE MARGINS

There was a long message on my answering machine when I got home. It was hilarious. From Paul and Ron. A conference call from their offices. Wanted to know if I would join them for dinner at the Mexican restaurant down the street before our Course group tonight. I guess the word is getting out that I am officially separated. I doubt they have anything but honorable intentions, though sometimes I get some curious vibes off Paul. Like he's interested but is afraid to make any moves. Maybe he corralled Ron to ease him into the picture? It would be safe. Not like a date. No personal rejection if I declined. Or, perhaps I am just so love starved that I'm imagining his interest. At any rate, I met them and we had a nice time.

After the meeting, the group planned a fiesta to christen Emily's new deck – and an ice cream "with all the fixings" movie night at Cliff and Natalie's. Things are looking up.

INTO THE WHITE • JOURNAL
Meditation, Wednesday Morning, May 4

Meditated for over forty minutes. Asked the Holy Spirit and my guides to join me. Also thought to include my Higher Self, whom I now call Big B!

Flashbacks of the cottage at Lakeville in 1977. So many feelings washing over me as I witness the two of us in all our glory, our best – falling so short. I am given a rag and told to "wipe clean" the images flashing before me, as I would a window. As I do, all colors disappear. There is only white. Like a freshly painted wall, except that it is bright and luminescent. A small box with a lid is placed in front of me and I'm told to put the soiled rag in the box.

Next, I am back at the little house in Royal Oak. The same kind of thing is happening, only this time Ray is observing with me. I'm given a fresh rag. After I've wiped the scenes clean, the box reappears and I drop the rag in. We step *into* the white that is left and sit for a while. It is very peaceful. This is our past. Our past is nothing! Opalescent green, yellow, and blue colors enfold us. Everything fades.

Presuming to be finished, I start to come out of the meditation, but I'm stopped short with images from our time in Stone Mountain. Same scenario. Flashbacks. Rapid fire feelings. Ray is still with me. I wipe the images clean and drop my rag in the box. This time, I look down as my third rag vanishes. The box is bottomless! Like a laundry shoot into another dimension. All the rags have disappeared! We step into the white. Again, the images from our past feel empty. They are nothing.

I ask what could have held us together, if all that was meaningless. I get the impression of something existing through and yet apart from all that. Something created from our union, but with a life of its own. Something safe and contained. We could not, would not, have remained together were it not for that essence. It felt still. Peaceful. More real than all the past we had experienced.

As I bring myself out and thank Ray for joining me in Spirit I wonder why the meditation didn't start in New York with our first two years of marriage. I feel at peace.

JOURNAL • Wednesday, 2:00 p.m.

I am getting bogged down in details. Again. Tuesday was such a good day. I felt trusting. My work with Sandra continues to validate the acceleration. Look at what has transpired in just six weeks. This shift in perception is awesome.

So, why have I allowed myself to get weighted down with all these mundane concerns? "What will happen to me if Ray consolidates his credit? Should we put our house in Oxford on the market? Are people judging us poorly for the choices we've made?" Like I can figure this out! The decisions I would make, heading toward divorce, might be very different from the decisions I would make with a reconciliation in the wind.

Fear comes rearing its ugly head when I think that Ray may consolidate his bills, leaving me out in the cold with cash advances for his business showing on my credit. Who is to know? It's his word against mine. My insistence on separate credit identities, separate checking accounts, so we wouldn't argue over money once he got sober, sure feels like a set-up now – inviting in all kinds of attack and self punishment thoughts. I don't want this. The credit issue is ego's way of slipping my guilt "out of the box" and, once again, projecting it onto Ray.

"How could I have been so stupid? How could he do this to me? He never loved me. He just used me." I need to put all of this back in the box. That is my only task at the moment. These mental gymnastics will change nothing. I trust the Holy Spirit to handle the rest and inform me of any changes in what I am to do.

Ego says, "You can't do that. The Holy Spirit doesn't care about these material concerns. Go ahead and trust Spirit with spirit stuff, but let *me* handle these earthly details."

It's as if ego is stirring up these thoughts to deter me from doing the special meditation that Sandra and I talked about.

"Melding realities in a meditation? Who are you kidding? What makes you think Ray has a Higher Self to connect with? Or that you could even do it, if he did? How stupid! What if he shows up at the door? What then? Look at his stuff! He is going to screw you! He will dump you and run off with Shelly anyway. Then won't you feel dumb for doing all these visualizations? You can't create anything. You didn't make this world or its rules. You don't have any real power. Melding realities! The Big Guy will punish you for that. The best thing you can do now is hide. You are flawed and at the mercy of circumstances *because* you're flawed. There's no shift. You and Sandra really are in a dream world."

Bingo! The first truthful statement ego has made! This *is* a dream world.

Something real clicked in, when I was with Sandra. I *felt* the divine guidance in everything that I had been doing. I felt the healing as *now*, not waiting for Ray and me to get back together. That is the shift, and I still feel it!

Holy Spirit, please don't let go. Even if I drag my feet. Maybe I only trust You because I see no better choice at the moment. In truth, I know there is no *other* choice. "Nothing real can be threatened, nothing unreal exists?"* Which is which? Show me what is real. Guide me through this – rapidly! So be it.

OUT OF THE BOX • JOURNAL • Thursday, May 5

Ray called this morning about his conversation with Howard regarding our business loan agreement. He wanted to come over tonight to work out the wording on the new contract, but I had already decided I was going to do my special meditation. We agreed to set up another time to take care of the contract business, but he was still insistent on dropping off the check for Howard and picking up his mail. Don't know what this will do to my plans. Not too sure about answering the door. Maybe I will just leave his mail in the box on the porch. Guess I'll know what to do when the time comes.

When I asked him what he'd told Howard about us, he said that he had not mentioned Shelly. Only that we'd been separated for two months and that it had not been an abrupt decision.

That wording gets me and I need to look at why. That he perceives his behavior as "not abrupt" bugs the hell out of me. How does "not abrupt" tie into my investment of guilt? How does it let my guilt out of the box? Ego wants to say it *was* abrupt because that takes me off the hook and puts him on. Somehow, *abrupt* makes it his fault. Makes him look flaky and irresponsible. He is guilty, not I. But if I did not already fear that I was guilty, his wording wouldn't

---

*A Course in Miracles (Temecula, CA, 1985, Foundation for *A Course in Miracles*)

bother me. I would not get back into the tirades of "How dare he call her, after all these years, on an impulse, and say it was not abrupt! Look at what he did! At what he's doing!"

I'm right back into all my original guilt and punishment stuff. Good Lord, is it even possible to keep my guilt in the box? I'm trying to be vigilant. But I keep wanting him to be accountable to his self-deception, and in wanting that perhaps I deceive myself. I know ego is trying to make me angry so I will cancel this meditation tonight. What if Ray and I really do connect, soul to soul? I'm getting in touch with some fear here. Fear that I could not live with this separation, knowing the depth of my love for him – or how great is the love we share. Could knowing this destroy me? Isn't it better to keep my distance? Better to be angry?

I'm seeing a parallel. Why I might be afraid to *really* know God's love. Where my guilt comes from, in believing that I would be capable of turning from One so dear. What a horrendous soul I must be to have abandoned a Love so great for a world like this. How could I have even thought to "eat the apple"? My grief is ancient. This separation from God is my doing – my fault. And the damage is irreparable. Therefore, any reminder of His love would only send me writhing in pain for what I can never know again. And that kind of pain *would* destroy me. Better to hide. Better to keep my distance. Better to be angry.

I'm seeing this everywhere. I fear God's love. Ray's love. My love. I fear love, period! What a place to be in! I'm afraid to remember that I intimately *know* this Love. So, what do I do with this? How can I *be* with this? Holy Spirit, cast some light on it. I am willing to look.

MELDING REALITIES MEDITATION
Thursday Night, May 5

Preparation started shortly after 9:00 p.m.. Candles and incense lit. Music on. Relaxation bath drawn. Wine poured. A perfect setting for a perfect "date."

Soaked in the tub for an hour, taking in all the sensory stimuli and going deep into relaxed meditation. The phone rang. A hang-up. Maybe Ray? I patted myself dry and went into the bedroom to put on the silk kimono I'd bought especially for this evening. How resistant I was to Sandra's suggestion that I pamper myself and shop for something so frivolous, considering my financial situation. And how shocked I was – my compromise being to buy only from the clearance rack – when the register rang up $2.25 for what I thought was a $22.50 purchase. Ten percent of the sale price! What an affirmation!

For the next part of my meditation, I settled comfortably into my usual cross-legged position on the bed. The crystal I felt drawn to pick up was in position. I noticed that it had four points. Two small clear points to one side (little selves) and two large clear points to the other (Higher Selves) with a cloudy horizontal "bridge" between. I reflected on the symbolism. This would go to Ray. I decided I'd wrap it and put it in the box, to be picked up with the rest of his mail, after I finished.

I focused on surrender. I felt like crying. Loving memories passed before me. I felt honored to have done all I had for Ray and was grateful for all he had done for me. I thought about the first time we met and how far he'd traveled to find me. A "me" that had given up on men – working for a company in the midst of bankruptcy – wondering what was going to happen next. I knew it was our Higher Selves that drew us together and, in part, kept us together through those years of "nothing."

I saw his strength in taking the hit for playing the bad guy in this separation. He did this so I could have more. So *we* could have more. I saw the teacher in him. I felt love for him. I felt love from him.

I asked that some aspect of his Higher Self join me in meditation and remain with me through the night – and for a sign that we'd made the connection. So Be It.

JOURNAL • Friday Morning, May 6

Shock of shocks! I went to place Ray's crystal in the box on the porch with his other mail and found all his stuff gone and a check for the business loan. When had he come? Why didn't he knock? Why hadn't I checked the box before I went to sleep last night?

Okay, all I need to know is that he was on the porch exactly when he was supposed to be, and that he had to be around the energy of last night's meditation. The crystal is still his, but apparently not to be given to him yet.

I will trust the Holy Spirit and our Higher Selves. He's on his way back.

JOURNAL • Saturday Night, May 7

Sandra and Adam's wedding reception was this afternoon. Was hit with the oddest feeling when I stepped out onto my porch. Emotional turmoil just poured over me, drenched me, like in a slap stick comedy where a pail of water dumps over a poor unsuspecting soul from the top of a door. Only this did not feel like a comedy. Somewhere, the bottom fell out.

I'd felt fine in the house. Had just finished wrapping their present and was looking forward to celebrating with them. Wondered if this was an omen that I shouldn't go. Did a gut check and felt like it really wasn't any of my stuff. By the time I got to the party, the feeling was gone. Have no idea what it was.

Sandra was appreciative of my willingness to attend. Had a good time. Lots of folks I knew. Some had heard the news of our separation and expressed their concern. It really didn't throw me. I was glad to be there.

Got into a conversation about lucid dreaming with a fellow who had hosted a small meditation group that Ray and I had attended a few times. It was kind of cute. He had no memory of meeting me, though he seemed to remember

Ray. Actually, he reminded me of a younger Ray. His girlfriend did not seem to be happy that we were talking. She's supposed to be some well-known psychic in the area. You'd think she would have picked up that I was not a threat. I definitely know that he was only into the conversation. I was as invisible to him as I am to Ray. Really didn't appreciate the psychic daggers shot my way. Hurt my feelings at first. Fed my victim stuff, I guess. Couldn't she see I was already wounded? Ha! Wanted to tell her, if I was having to deal with my insecurities, she should deal with hers. Don't pass them off on me!

And I definitely have no interest in repeating a younger version of Ray!

IN THE MARGINS

Had my first taste of Thai food – in the Highlands – with The Course gang. Fell in love with it. Never much cared for iced tea of any kind but Natalie urged me to try the Thai tea. God, I think I'm hooked.

Called Samantha when I got home. She is still wanting me to meet her friend. Maybe I will suggest this restaurant for our blind date.

JOURNAL • Monday, 4:30 a.m., May 9

Two dreams about Ray. We were in the Highlands to see Josh, Ray's acting coach, and his fiancee perform as clowns. We had to move some heavy boxes into a back room before the show. When we finished, I commented to Ray that Shelly would not have helped him with carrying that load. Just as I was thinking, "God, why did I say that? I should have kept my mouth shut," Ray said, "You're right, she wouldn't have."

It felt like we were on a date and Shelly was out of the picture, though Ray had not committed to revealing that yet.

We went out front, to enjoy the performance and eat.

Food was cafeteria style. Lea was there. As we were going through the dessert line, she joked about my fruit being in the same container as always. Ray did not feel close in this dream – but also did not feel so distant. Distracted maybe. Inattentive because he was doing a lot of mental sorting out.

I woke up. Couldn't get back to sleep, so I recited the verse from The Course, "Nothing real can be threatened. Nothing unreal exists. Herein lies the peace of God."* I have been using that a lot when I'm restless at night. Puts me to sleep faster than counting sheep. Maybe it's God's peace taking over or maybe ego just knocks me out to avoid the prayer.

My next dream. Ray and I were at a wedding in an old English Tudor mansion. Lea was there again. The wedding seemed to be a surprise. People were scurrying about. Still planning and preparing for the ceremony. I wondered if we were early. We wandered around and found food set out on tables – in what we assumed to be the reception area – in the garden of a small cottage across the street. I fixed a plate for Ray and me to share, while we waited for them to get their act together.

ONE WHO KNOWS • DREAM • May 10

I came to a cliff's edge on the top of a mountain. The way down was long and arduous. There were people with me, but I was to be the first to go down. A guide, who held two ropes on a pulley, instructed me not to let go of the rope I was holding. As I started the frightening trek down, I heard a voice say, "Let the one who knows guide you. You will get down much faster."

It was a fantastic descent when I just relaxed with it. As if we were flying. Buoyant. Landing, then bouncing and jumping, and flying some more. When we got safely to the bottom, I looked up. Where I had come from was so far away, it was not even perceivable. I was charged! I wanted

---

A Course In Miracles (Temecula, CA, 1985, Foundation for A Course in Miracles)

to go back up with the guide to get the others. It felt like Ray was in the group, waiting. They were all very busy, gathering what they would need to prepare for their descent. My Mom was with them, trying to retrieve some vintage fabric I hadn't had time to pack. There was a lot of snow, again.

THE PURPLE DOOR • JOURNAL
Tuesday, 2:30 p.m., May 10

Sitting in the showroom. I hear music playing across the hall, songs that make me think of us, and find I am missing the *future*. I need to be careful about projecting that I should miss a future with Ray. I guess it's progress, in that I am not letting memories from the past drag me down.

I see so many possibilities for Ray and me. Especially with the insights this separation is bringing. I don't see him with Shelly for long, though sometimes fear and guilt step in. Heart says, "Don't worry. What they have won't work." Fear says, "Are you kidding? Even if it doesn't, he would rather be alone and single than be with you!" That's my punishment stuff. My core belief, guilt stuff. I don't need to be afraid if he chooses to be alone. It is not a reflection of my worthiness.

I find myself cleaning up the entrance to my little bungalow. Planting impatiens on either side of the old brick steps, spreading fresh bales of pine straw – God, I love the smell of pine needles – pruning the bushes along the walkway, and obsessing on finding the perfect purple to paint my screen door. As if to say, "Hey world, look at me emerging from the ashes!" The poor guy at the paint store could probably have done with seeing less of me. Polite exasperation with a tinge of curiosity was *his* hue when I showed up for the third time with quart in hand. According to him, the base could not take any more pigment and I was going to have to start over from scratch or settle. I am pretty sure I detected a sigh of relief when I decided to go with what I had. It still doesn't match the purple I see in my head, but my door is a big hit with Angie's kids.

I feel the shift has occurred and is making its way to consciousness and the physical realm. Thus the quest for my perfectly expressive door!

Holy Spirit, take my fears and guilts, and cleanse them. I see how my negative core is based on guilt, just as The Course says. How that feeling of unworthiness, that fear of punishment, connects to a belief that I'm guilty for something. I remember uncovering this years ago in my first inventory and fifth step. As far back as I could remember, I felt afraid. As far back as I could remember, I felt guilty. Even before kindergarten! So many childhood nights spent lying in bed, crying, "Why am I here? This is a mistake!" Feeling banished, abandoned, punished! For what, I did not know. I have always wondered how one so young could have such intense feelings of guilt and fear before life experiences justified them.

Ego was prominent right from the start. Something in me grieved. But for what? I only knew there was something I was sad for. Someplace else to be. I spent most of my time working very hard to cover up that guilt – the defectiveness that banished me to this place – discovering early on that "performance" masked that lack, to some degree. If I just kept things stirred up, I could outrun that awful feeling.

Thank God for *The Course in Miracles* and my special relationship with Ray coming to a freeze, or I would never have seen this. Matthew almost showed me. Actually, the abrupt ending of that relationship did reveal my self-hatred, but I couldn't stand it and had to go into hiding with men. One sick, distracting relationship after another. That glimpse was so devastating, it has taken me nineteen years to get back to it. And now I look only because I am conscious of a connection with something greater than myself that will help me through.

SPIRIT DIALOG • Tuesday, May 10

I feel like I'm not going to make it to June the fourteenth. The emotional roller coaster is intense. The pain of missing Ray. The thoughts that I'm still sharing him with Shelly. The fear that he moved in with her this weekend. I feel wracked from one end of the spectrum to the other. If I am creating my reality with *these* thoughts, I'm scared. It's a mess! I feel far away from you guys. I'm even afraid to do the writing. Ego is saying I made it all up. That you can't give me specifics. God, I want relief. Now! And, right now, I spell relief, R.A.Y. Help me.

Keep looking through the eyes of The Course. It will help you to keep the belief in guilt to the forefront, where it will cause you less harm. You will not be able to be rid of it here but you do not get punished for believing in guilt, as your ego would have you fear. Why would a God, who knows you as guiltless, punish you for guilt you **think** *you have? Is that not absurd?*

You will make it through this. You still fall back into your fear that Ray is having a great time with Shelly. How many times need we tell you it will not last. When she is gone, you will come up to surface in his heart. You will be there in a way that you have never been before, as he is in your heart differently as well. There is not much else you can do beyond what you are already doing. Keep the vigil.

Trust your feelings. Trust yourself, as well as us. The writing is good but so much work for us to merely repeat what you already know.

Thank you for these words.

JOURNAL • Wednesday, May 11

Written in showroom: Had a strong image come to me in this morning's visualization. Sitting on the front porch steps, I saw Ray walking up the driveway with a bouquet of flowers. His eyes were twinkling. I knew he was coming home. We wept. We hugged. He said, "I love you." Smitty was at the door, purring. Ray cradled him in his arms the way he used to. We were a family again.

Somewhere, in the midst of this meditation, Smitty did an odd thing. He crawled onto my lap and started kneading my thigh with his paws. Very gently and consistently. He settled into a nap position and remained there until I was through with my meditation. Did he know something? Could he feel the energy?

I don't understand how I can be feeling so panicky now, with a meditation like that starting my day. I called Sandra. Her 9:00 a.m. canceled, so I was able to get a thirty minute session on the phone. She pointed out that I was back into my black and white mode. That's what it feels like. All or nothing. Hot or cold. I've got no tepid. Just like during the first two weeks. The anger ripples to the surface and surprises me with its sense of urgency to carry out some fantastical plot of revenge. My ego screams for something dramatic, like hauling the rest of his belongings down from the attic and dumping them in the middle of the street to be flattened by traffic, following him to her place and letting the air out of his tires, or kicking him in the stomach – absolutely pummeling him. I know it's because I want the pain to stop and imagine that doing something so out of character might bring relief, even if only momentary.

Ego says, "Cut him off. He's betrayed you. He's guilty. Cut the ties and get on with your life. Then you'll be rid of the pain." Divide and conquer. The way of ego. Survival through separation. But I don't want to disconnect. Not from Ray. Not from God. Not from me. This way stinks! I want wholeness. I want love.

Ego says, "You shouldn't let yourself love that much. It will only hurt you. Devastate you. You've done all these meditations and what have they accomplished? Is Ray with you now? No! They've got you loving him more than ever.

Look at the pain loving him is causing you! You can't love something you're separated from. It hurts too bad. Isn't anger a better way to get through separation? Hatred. Anger. Punishment. That is what ends the pain. You are far too vulnerable. You better toughen up girl!"

Laura popped into the showroom a little while ago. She noted the strained look on my face. I told her I felt like I was reliving the first two weeks of March, and confessed to missing Ray. She suggested I might be empathing. Said that I was sensitive and may be tuning into his feelings. Is it possible that some of this "missing" is being shared?

Ego says, "Well, if that's the case, why isn't he calling you?"

If only there were some way I could find out for sure. He's not in a space to admit to second thoughts about Shelly or to leaving our marriage.

Wow, the angels are really taking care of me. Jan, from the new showroom down the hall, just stopped by and was insistent that I join her for lunch. Sandra. Laura. Jan. I'm not being allowed to go too far into my crazies today. I wonder if Smitty knew I would be in need of an extra dose of love and was trying to comfort me this morning.

JOURNAL • Wednesday, 3:20 p.m., May 11

I will not be punished for missing Ray. I will not be punished for loving Ray. I will not be punished for wanting Ray back. I will not be punished for fears connected to Ray. I will not manifest these fears because the love I hold for being with Ray is stronger than the fear I see for losing him.

Ego wants to turn it all into fear. This sadness is not always from fear. Some of this discomfort comes from what feels to be an unnatural state of separation and frustration. These are not punishable feelings. I don't need to manifest punishment for having these feelings. They are my call for love and that call will be answered. Is being answered.

So be it.

JOURNAL • Thursday, May 12

Written in showroom: Meditation was at 8:00 a.m.. Smitty joined me. He kneaded only a little, before settling in next to me. I focused on sending love to Ray. I felt one strong surge of energy run through me. Like an eruption. The rest was a gentle flow.

My mind wandered to Paul, then Eric. Spirit encouraged me to see that my attraction for Paul is in response to his projections toward me – and that if Eric were to project the same, I would be responsive to him as well – and that if Ray were to, I would be ecstatic! I could see where my sensitivity to other's feelings, and my responsiveness to their projections causes confusion. I take these as my thoughts and feelings when many times they're not. I am only empathing. Like Laura said. Definitely something to consider. I can see where this goes way back – into my childhood.

Next, my mind wandered to an old girlfriend that Ray used to talk about. Felt like this tied to Shelly somehow. Are these Ray's connections? Is Spirit trying to tell me something? They could be saying not to worry because Ray, in telling me about her, was very clear about the unhealthy patterns in that relationship and his desire not to repeat it in *any* form.

As soon as I finished my meditation, the phone rang. Picked up on two rings before really thinking. It was Ray! I was still kind of spacey so I don't remember the initial reason he gave for calling but, somewhere in there, he said, "I feel like I'm forgetting something." It struck me as odd that he would call at that particular moment. He could have waited until payday, as the "forgetting" ultimately had to do with bills of course. But the wording and timing struck me as having more to do with my projection to him. Like a "forgetting" interpreted from something missing. Like me! We agreed that he would come over Sunday evening to discuss our financial business.

Show me how to get him to see me *as I am*.

Show different. Be different. Dress different. Have a glass of wine in his presence. Play a New York album. New incense. Sit on the front porch with your purple door. He will see a Bernadette he will be drawn to. When he thinks of this Bernadette with other men, it will bother him. He will be curious what this Bernadette will be like with them, and that they may experience something he did not. Do not confront. Do not challenge. Be in your female energy. Do not project your guilt. Do not withhold love.

I can handle it. These are all things that I am doing and enjoying now, without him. Thank you for his phone call. Whether I'm in a fantasy world or not, it gave me hope. I do love him. I do love us. And I am trying to love me.

SACRED SPARKS • JOURNAL • Friday, May 13

Written in showroom: 8:00 a.m. meditation. Visualized my path to Ray as open, traveling both ways. I focused on my heart, not my head. I thought to pull energy in and was told, "No. Pull it *out*." That to "pull in" from what I know is to pull from nothing, as there is nothing out there to pull in from! Is this an exercise in creation? Extension? Is it from this point that Ray and I are one?

The field was activated to open all memory banks regarding him and me, in this lifetime, in these forms. I watched him come up the porch steps. I allowed the joy to flow through me as I welcomed him home.

Then I saw us, sitting on the floor. Face to face, my legs wrapped around his waist. We were sitting very still, looking deeply into each other's eyes. In this part of the meditation, I actually started to feel pulsations. Energy rising from below the base of my spine. I felt it expanding with each pulse. Through my solar plexus, my heart, and throat. I did not feel the pulsations as strongly when they traveled through my crown, but it was clear the journey was complete. I saw the same progression happening for Ray. Like powerful fireworks between us, with no sound or outer movement to stand as evidence of what was happening. Emoting was intense.

DREAM

Ray and I were in an old car. Ray was driving. We were behind a new jeep, which Ray was *also* driving – with another woman. We were supposed to follow them. The other woman did not feel like Shelly. Was it I? Anyway, they turned left into a shopping plaza while we kept driving past. I told Ray we missed our turn. Frustrated, I asked him why he always had to go too far. He made a U-turn and headed back to the parking lot where they sat waiting for us. I awakened.

IN THE MARGINS

Talked with Mom. Peggy is pregnant. She and William can barely make ends meet with the two girls. I don't know how they'll do it with a third. Mom said Peg was really struggling with it the day she found out. That would have been last Saturday, when Sandra and Adam had their reception. Wow. The awful feelings that hit me when I stepped out onto my porch that day were hers.

IN THE MARGINS

Saturday's ice cream and movie night at Cliff and Natalie's was a success. What a creative spread! Our "kids" went to town! Every topping we could imagine – and then some. Ice cream was just the blank canvas onto which we poured a multi-colored, textural palette of dietary delights! It has been a long, long time since I've had sweets. I don't even keep them in the house since Ray left. It was fun, eating as much as I wanted without feeling guilty. One benefit of losing so much weight!

I supplied the whipped cream. Someone started joking about the many creative ways to use it, and we were off and running. Had to be careful. Got a little worked up with Paul being there! A challenging combination of too much sugar and no sex. Who am I kidding? I don't need to pin that on Paul. Or the sugar. My hormones are raging. At my peak, and alone. Well at least I can feel safe in the group. We might joke, but there is always a sense of honor for each other.

Got a lot out of Sunday's Course meeting. Really feel like I am integrating the text. Maybe a better word would be internalizing. This all feels very personal. It's as if Ray and I are in the middle of acting out a living demonstration of what these pages are talking about. And our acting out is helping me to see that The Course has a real and practical application. Not just something to intellectually dissect or banter about. "What does this paragraph or that sentence really mean?" Hell, it's quite clear when the head *and* heart are as involved as mine are. I am raw. I am living it. I am getting it!

A few of us went to the log cabin, afterward, for breakfast. Natalie confessed to playing mental matchmaker. Seems she thinks that the guy who is chairing Sunday's Course meetings would be a good possibility for me, should I start dating. She is not too far off base. He does score high on the right side of the column.

Funny. We all know that automatically substituting a new relationship for an old one that fails is not always the most successful solution. Kind of a take-off on the old hangover cure that advocates the "hair of the dog that bit you." In pain? Just don't come down from the high. Bloody Marys and Sunday brunch. A socially acceptable remedy for a Saturday night gone too far. An odd cure, to extend the behavior that brought our misery. And yet, when it comes to relationship woes, we can hardly resist the temptation to fill the gap.

Stopped at the tanning salon after breakfast. Was in a good space when I got home so I decided to change out the shelf paper in the bathroom and hang a few new pictures. Somewhere in doing that I started to feel like crying. Out of nowhere. God, what an awful feeling! The sadness was intense and washed over me in waves. It didn't connect with anything appropriate to where I was. Just raw emotion. I couldn't shake it. Even called Peggy to see if I was empathing any of her stuff, but she was fine.

RESCUED • JOURNAL • Tuesday, 3:30 p.m., May 17

Had another good meditation this morning. Smitty joined me. It is so sweet, sharing those moments with him. This time, I saw a doorway, and was told to consider that is all the body represents. A doorway is neutral when its function is merely to act as a passage through. Contemplating my body in this way gave me an odd feeling. Almost a little unnerving.

Then I saw myself as a swinging door, like those you see in restaurant kitchens. Swinging. One room – heaven – the real world. The other room – here – the dream world. As long as I identify with the body, I am like that door – swinging from one room, one world, into the other. So, I wonder, if this body is just a door, who or what is doing the swinging? And from where? What are the feelings and judgments that swing me? How do I choose the room – the world I most want to experience?

This morning, I had my scheduled session with Sandra but my car wouldn't start. So, I cranked up the old Volare, that I'd not driven in months, and headed for Covington. About fifteen miles out I looked down at the dashboard, just in time to see the temp gage rising fast. I pulled off at the next exit and coasted into a convenience store lot, feeling frustrated. Most everyone I knew would be at work and I didn't have the money for a tow truck. I called Ray's Mom and she picked me up.

I decided I'd call Ray when I got to her place. Don't know what I thought he could, or would, do. Guess I figured if I was stranded, he might as well know about it and suffer with me, though I was sure not to come across that way on the phone. Turns out it was his day off and he was just heading out to do his laundry. He picked me up and we headed back to my car with two jugs of water. He wanted to see if the Volare could make it back home. Said he would follow me.

His demeanor was different. More open, though still cautious. Made small talk. Commented on the car he'd bought from the dealership where he was working. Said he had tried to find a deal on an automatic so I could borrow it if I wanted to go out of town. Something more reliable than what I'm driving now. I wonder if that's true.

I thanked him for coming to my rescue and assured him that I did not plan on making a habit of calling him, that I would start handling these emergencies myself. He said I should not hesitate to call him whenever I needed help. Very different from the man who, only weeks ago, suggested I start finding another emergency support system.

After he poured in the second gallon of water, he stopped and remarked on how nicely my turquoise necklace matched the blouse I was wearing. Then he gave me a big, out-of-the-blue hug, saying how good I looked and how glad he was to see me. It came so fast I had no response, except to return the hug and say thank you. It shocked me. And I think it even surprised him.

The Volare made it all the way home with no overheating. I parked it in the driveway and he drove me to the train station. I totally blew my appointment with Sandra and did not want to miss work too. He insisted I have Angie pick me up rather than try to walk from the station after work. I almost argued but a voice said, "Hush!" I joked that he'd have good karma the rest of the day for being a knight in shining armor, and asked if I could thank him with a kiss on the cheek. He teased that I wouldn't catch anything if I kissed him on the lips. I told him I didn't know what protocol was. He didn't either. So, I kissed him. Once on the cheek. Twice on the lips. What the hell. Told him to have a good day. Had to focus on *not* saying "I love you," either from habit or feeling. It left an odd vacuum. I don't know if he felt it too. He didn't let on if he did.

Okay guys, who manifested two cars breaking down so Ray would have the opportunity to rescue me? Is this more of your work? I don't believe in coincidences. When he said, "Where are your angels? I thought they would keep your cars running," and I mused that you were off somewhere else, my heart knew you were right where you were supposed to be – with an agenda to thwart the vehicles today. Curious how the Volare got all the way back with no overheating (with only water, not even anti-freeze). And who told me to look at the temp gage when I did, so I would be ready for it and not miss the most convenient exit to his mother's?

Perhaps you thought Ray would find some value in "doing for me" while I would find value in "receiving from him"?

JOURNAL • Same Day, 11:44 p.m.

Ray dropped by with the check for the business loan. He'd spent the rest of the afternoon with his mother. Was self-absorbed and distracted. Not the same man who helped with my car today or who dropped me off at the train station. He talked about his job and his roommate, Charles. No questions. No hugs. No kisses. But I'm okay with that. I know Ray's Higher Self got him to call first and see if I was still up. He could have just slipped by and stuck the check in the box, as we'd agreed earlier. All is in divine order.

SPIRIT DIALOG • Tuesday, May 24

Tonight was Course study at Cliff and Natalie's. Stopped by Ray's, on the way. Figured it would be a safe time to drop off his mail because he'd be at work. Easy in. Easy out. Wrong. His schedule had changed. When he walked out to greet me, I noticed that he wasn't wearing her friendship ring. I should have thought better than to ask him about it.

We got into a conversation in the driveway. Some of the things he said really got under my skin. I drove off with an uneasy feeling. Couldn't concentrate on what the group was discussing so I left early. I knew that would concern Cliff and Natalie because they knew where I had been, but I couldn't wait to excuse or explain myself. I had to get at some honesty with Ray. Wasn't sure how I would do it. Prayed hard for guidance as I headed back to his place.

He doesn't see the mirrors. It's obvious that Shelly's rather difficult personality is challenging him to look hard at himself, but he's looking through the chaotic filter of *their* relationship, just as Spirit has said. He is hurting over *her* abruptness in breaking off their five week affair. I'm hurting over *his* abruptness in breaking off our eighteen year marriage! I sensed no empathy from him when I took advantage of the opportunity to draw that parallel. It was all about her – and about his feelings.

Then, as if that weren't enough, I found out that my recent episode of Sunday afternoon blues came from him! Can't get him to connect with *my* feelings but I sure can get his. Damn! He'd gone to the Unity church where we used to go – looking for comfort. He spent most of Sunday afternoon crying – lost – feeling the depth of his separation and isolation – from God – from everything. Damn! It doesn't seem fair. Sunday afternoon was awful for me, and the feelings I was having weren't even mine!

Somewhere in our talking, I decided to practice vulnerability with Ray (per my sessions with Sandra) in the spirit of absolute honesty. Did not conceal any of my cards. Really tried to own my stuff and not hide behind a good-guy-bad-guy script. Told him I was working hard at not projecting my guilt onto him. About how my fears kept me from asking for what I needed in the relationship – and how I used his acting career, our business ventures, his struggle with depression, as excuses for postponing those needs.

He apologized for what had happened between us. He said, "For what it's worth." I let him know that his apology had worth to me. That we're not as separate as our egos would like us to think. That we still impact each other.

Then the biggie. I told him I still loved him. Admitting that to him was the most challenging expression of vulnerability. One for which I am now under vicious ego attack.

Ego says, "How could you be so stupid? Why did you tell him that? He didn't say it back. He won't say it back. He obviously doesn't love you. That just showed you *both* how stupid you are – and you, how unworthy. Your call for love will not be answered – except with evidence of your guilt! And that is too damn vulnerable!"

I'm so pumped up. It's almost 1:00 a.m. The memory of our talk feels disjointed and scattered. No matter how out of sequence, I have to get down what I can remember.

He admitted to hoarding resentments toward me.

I admitted to seeing that we wanted the same things. To seeing how our lack of courage in taking certain emotional risks kept us from being able to pursue those things within our marriage.

God, I even talked about how my fear of expressing passion and spontaneity in our sex life ultimately took its toll on my ability to express as an artist. How I couldn't protect myself, in accommodating his depression or the challenges his medication presented, by shutting down in one area and not have it affect the other.

I told him I believed there had been a lot of talk but no true communication between us. That we'd been in a relationship for eighteen years and knew nothing about *how* to be in a relationship. That I believed there had to have been something very present and real between us to have made it this long.

I have to continue clarifying communications with Ray. No more enabling. Make him look. Make him question his own motives. "Why are you calling me? What do you want from me?"

I think I might still slap him for making me walk on eggshells these past six years while he kept her on the pedestal.

So, what am I to make of tonight? Is there anything more you can tell me about the next few months? Truth or nothing!

You saw a man who still has a way to go. Who still does not honor himself and so cannot honor you. He does not yet see, but he will soon. You must stay out of the way. Yes, be diligent in recognizing which of these feelings is yours and which are his. When you do your meditations you do not close the door and so his feelings come back to you. It is okay for the door to be open if you would but recognize what is yours and what is not. Laura speaks true. Protect yourself.

Getting out of town for a little while would be good. It will be timely for you to go.

You have freedom to date. It will help you to be sure, as well, that Ray is for you and that you are not looking to him out of fear. There could be a casual exchange between you and Eric. He is curious about you. He is drawn to your strength. Let him know where it comes from. It will challenge him.

Ray will be back. This you know in your heart, which is why you maintain room for him. Be patient. It is okay to love him still, as your husband. He will come to know the value of your union and will choose it over many possibilities, real or imagined. Ha! He will know love for you again.

We know this time seems long, but listen to Sandra. It will collapse into nothing, and is so necessary for your process. It had to be this way.

Are we not doing well in our assessments? You might come to trust this information, no? Trust. A new experience for you? So new, you do not even recognize when you are having it!

Love and Light. Rest in peace, child.

JOURNAL • Friday, 6:30 a.m., May 27

A dream: Ray and I were visiting his cousins. Lots of people were around. Ray disappeared. I needed to get to work. I felt cool and irritated toward him. I found him with Shelly. Her head hung down. They were sitting on a bed. He had just finished making love to her. I thought, "The nerve! And here among family!" He had his arm around her. I took the only set of keys for the car, knowing he would have no transportation later. I was calm. Even said, "Pleased to meet you, Shelly," as I left. She wouldn't look up. I was wearing my funky white silk dress with a conservative blazer over the top. I planned to remove the blazer later in the evening, to go out dancing.

I think this dream means I am not going to wait for Ray. I'm going on with my life – thus the car keys. In the dream, he was oblivious and unresponsive to what my departure would mean – as he is now, still thinking he can cater to her in my presence. Could this dream be supporting my decision to date, and to get more of Ray's stuff out of here?

IN THE MARGINS

So, could Eric and I really get away with a "casual exchange"? How casual is casual, I wonder. A kiss? More, perhaps? Would that even be possible? We've known each other for so long. God, my hormones are running so wild I can't even think clearly. I know how I could relieve this pressure but I just can't move in that direction. My only choice is to keep channeling this sexual energy into my meditations.

THE KISS • JOURNAL • Sunday, May 29

    Well, casual is a kiss. And, as I relive last night with Eric, it does not feel so casual as it does complicated. It was a great evening with a good friend. Had dinner. Went back to his place. We talked about passion and creativity. About eggshell walking in our marriages. Shared all kinds of things. When I got up to head home, it just happened. Was it him? Was it me? Went to hug and kiss good-bye like we have for years – but not quite like that. Damn. He is a good kisser. Doesn't surprise me. And he is kind. I can't stand this. I can't get over feeling like a charity case.

JOURNAL • Rune Drawing, Tuesday, May 31[*]

    I cannot stop thinking about that kiss. About what would happen if a sexual dimension were added to our relationship, so I've decided to draw three Runes for some insight and guidance:

    The first Rune represents the place I am now. I drew *Possessions*. This Rune speaks of finding nourishment as I travel from a place of mundane concerns to spiritual fulfillment, and it references the ancient phrase "as above so below." It says to conserve what I have gained. To be vigilant and mindful. It talks about looking deeply at what has meaning in my life. To look with care at what is required for my well-being. Is it truly in my best interest to *acquire* happiness through things or manipulated outcomes – or to continue working on myself? I have to admit this Rune is accurate in describing where my focus is now.

    The second Rune tells me the action or attitude required as I contemplate this hypothetical situation with Eric. I pulled the Rune of *Self*. This Rune emphasizes that anything of value must start with me and that I must be sure that what I am pursuing is in correct relationship with my self. If

---

[*]Rune drawing paraphrased from Ralph Blum, *The Book of Runes* (New York, 1987, Oracle Books / St. Martin's Press)

it is not, how can I hope to have a satisfying relationship with anyone else? It says that I must remain receptive to guidance from the Divine, to be in the world but not of it. It says I should live the ordinary life in an extraordinary way. That this is not a time for me to focus on results but rather to focus on the task at hand – on the process of growth and reparation. And above all that I should not be careless. I see nothing here that encourages pursuing Eric beyond the friendship.

The third Rune represents the outcome if I follow the second Rune's guidance. I pulled *Signals*. The key word for *Signals* is receiving. It says that I have to be open to receiving messages, signs, and gifts. That I have to integrate my unconscious motives – my core belief work – with conscious intent, to be diligent in my awareness. So what *are* my intentions? *Signals* points to connecting with God's inexhaustible resources, to accepting a calling to a new life, to looking for the unexpected. If I continue to nourish myself, there will be plenty to share. The most hopeful message of this Rune is that it affirms a newfound sense of family solidarity.

This reading does not seem to point to "go for it." It's more like a validation to sit tight and continue doing what I've been doing.

JOURNAL • Tuesday Evening

Free flow thoughts and feelings, resulting from kissing Eric.

- I am a charity case. He really did not want to kiss me but felt sorry for me. I repulsed him.
- He will be turned off by me, and we'll have to go through that awkward rejection stuff. He'll avoid me, or put me off.
- A good way to screw up a good friendship. Eric will lose respect for me.
- Sex *and* friendship. I can't successfully have both.

- Damn you, Ray, for leaving me out here in this single world. If I can't handle a kiss between old friends what am I going to be like with a new man? I am not equipped for this.
- I have never claimed responsibility for choosing passion. I've always laid claim to it through insane off-the-cuff moments. I'm afraid of my passion because it gets me into trouble and makes me vulnerable. There is no way to predict or control the outcome. Look where Ray's has led him.
- Things will get complicated. Eric will make me lose focus. Distract me from my visualizations, meditations, and lucid dreaming.
- I don't have faith that the Holy Spirit will handle these details while I go through this "casual" growth exchange. Why do I always think I am the one who has to keep the watchful eye?

> *Your anger comes from fear. Work with the fears. You are not so sad now, as you are afraid.*

> *Find your fear, and so your guilt hiding behind it.*

JUNE

ALTAR OF TRUTH • JOURNAL • Wednesday, 11:00 a.m., June 1

PMS day! Worst I've had since this whole separation business started. All I can do is write.

Ray really surprised me last night when he pulled into Cliff and Natalie's driveway before The Course meeting. Said he had something he wanted to tell me, then smiled and gave me a big hug. God, the gamut of emotions that ran through me! Then the news. He had been looking for another place to live and crossed paths with a guy he knew, through his acting circle, who was doing the same. They'd found an apartment and had just signed a six month lease. I was speechless. God, why? Six months. Six months and a legal document locking it in. Felt myself going numb. Got lost on the other side of a wall I couldn't break down. The *only* feeling I could get in touch with was annoyance at him for smoking a damn cigar while he related this to me. A passive aggressive display of his independence. How weird it was to be so in touch with feelings over something as petty as that stupid cigar while going numb to everything else!

Was exhausted when I woke this morning. Wanted to hide out for the day and have someone hold me, just hold me. I felt open and vulnerable. Absolutely raw. Feelings were running through me like a river – rapids from which I'd taken a few gulps and couldn't catch my breath. I was drowning. Lonely. The kind of loneliness that wasn't particular. Wasn't attached to needing any special somebody, so *any* body would do – as long as it was warm and could hold me.

When I look at Ray, I see his confusion. And I wonder: the longer he takes to sort things out and the more risks I take, at what point will I become more confused than he? I thought I had a direction, a certainty. But now I'm feeling I don't know much of anything. I am antsy, angry, absolutely worn out. I want to go someplace. Escape to the mountains. Visit my folks. Be *anywhere* but here feeling this! I want to call Ray and scream at him. Dump the rest of his stuff in the street. I want to get drunk, crawl into bed and disappear under the covers until all of this blows over.

Would have called in sick today if there had been someone to call in to. It's rough, managing the showroom on days like this. No one here to sub for me. A boss who lives out of state. I feel trapped. Isolated. The halls are empty. Not a single buyer and the morning is almost over.

This showroom looks so trashy. Everything I do to improve its appearance, Joel undoes when he comes through town. It never occurs to him to ask why I display product the way I do. My background in art and design, my understanding of color – all invisible to him. I am left to work around his chaotic hit and run arrangements. Replicas of antique guns and swords displayed with lace, doll house furniture, and Mother's day plaques! Good Lord. I need to find something to do that I will feel good about and appreciated for. My boss is just like Ray. What is it with these men? Am I so insignificant? Why do I reflect this back to myself?

God, I hate these cramps!

I can hear Aretha singing "R.E.S.P. E.C.T." on the radio in the showroom across the hall. That is what I want from Ray. No, actually – V. A.L.U.E. me! Ha! I want from him what I have not given myself. Maybe I have, up to a point. But I haven't looked hard enough at the *degree* of value. Like grading a diamond. I don't know my true worth. There are facets of me that I can only guess about.

Like my passion. Had I trusted myself. Had I been more willing to use the resources of my marriage to explore and expand that passion. Had I given myself permission to be that vulnerable, uncertain, imperfect with Ray. What would have happened? Would I have gained a greater sense of self worth? How many opportunities did I miss? All those times – pushed to the edge emotionally, spiritually, sexually with this man I said I would love and trust for better or worse. What was I afraid of discovering?

How do I get this on paper? Passion. Enthusiasm. Lust. For a partner? For living? Are they so different? Is the nature of our relationship with a partner evidence for our beliefs about life? Could the sexuality couples share *beyond* the honeymoon years be used as a tool to explore a more expansive, passionate sense of self? What a commitment that would be! Not easy. Even in a long term relationship, I see where such commitment could invite unnerving vulnerability. One would have to risk and *remain* at risk long after its expression. Ray and I chose to be safe in our familiarity, our friendship, our manipulative sex life. Damn. Passion, not lust. Chosen, risked for the *duration* of a relationship and not split off into some new love interest. Passion with honesty, intimacy, *and* friendship? What a challenge!

I don't know that I have ever allowed myself to experience passion and choice as synonymous. A conscious decision never appeared to be part of my equation. Passion was something that got me into trouble, got me hurt, or made me look stupid and out of control. It was something I craved but fell victim to – with painful consequences. Passion just never seemed to go well for me. Hell, there was no telling where you'd wind up when the dust settled. Swept away by a missionary calling, eating bugs in some foreign land, canonized a Saint, after being burned at the stake for a lethal combination of passion and angelic voices. Wouldn't it be insane to *choose* something that leads to that kind of uncertainty?

Look where it's gotten Ray. Shelly sparked his passion but now he's at risk, I'm at risk, and everybody is watching. But life without passion is a washout. Shades of gray. What a choice! Would fire have survived if, after discovering it, primitive man took it back to the safety of his cave and never left? Basic stuff.

The problem is the solution. Dare I choose passion? *Can I*? Could these seemingly uncontrollable roller coaster feelings be re-directed? Attached, instead, to honesty? Re-invested in vulnerability? Expressed, even at the risk of not knowing the outcome? Passion with accountability and no guarantees. Sacred and expansive. How do I get to know *this* kind of passion? Is there a forum where I can safely explore this now? Safely. There's that word. How would my need to control define "safely" this time?

Damn. This need to safely express passion is at the root of my block as an artist. I see it. I loved my art, but art was synonymous with poverty, and poverty was not my definition of safe. I had to make a living. My solution? Go into advertising. A good way to be a full time artist in a modern world. Compromise my creative autonomy for a guaranteed forty-plus-overtime. Innocent enough in the beginning. It seemed a secondary concern that I was expressing my creativity in a field that I had no interest in. Being in advertising kept me financially safe, and that safety justified continuing the emotional compromise that I had made. Passion or prostitution? Maintaining that status quo through the years meant distancing myself from creating anything that could spark any impassioned desire or yearning, any out-of-control feelings that would lead to unsafe behavior – like quitting my job. And, besides, being emotionally unattached to the subject matter or technique meant I never had to risk personal rejection when jobs bounced back for changes. (Boy, am I seeing a parallel with relationships here!)

How long has the artist in me grieved? I can't even glance at my drawing board or my tools (they used to be toys) without feeling remorse. That is, when I'm not just numb.

JOURNAL • Thursday, 6:00 a.m., June 2

There is virtually no part of my life that is as I thought it was. Motivations, intentions, what I thought I knew or understood about my art, my marriage, my identity. None of it! And as I look to honestly *see*, my life moves and shifts so swiftly that I cannot see *enough* to know what to do or where to begin – and yet, *they* say I've already begun!

"Look at yourself here, Bernadette. Look there, Bernadette. Did you know that was your real motivation, Bernadette?"

What you think you fear, you love. And what you love, you should think to fear. Protecting yourself from the very Force that is the Cause of your existence. Fearing It and loving that which would keep you lost.

JOURNAL • Thursday, 10:30 a.m., June 2

I see where Ray became my life, rather than came to be in my life. Somehow, I deluded myself into thinking that I was strong enough not to lose myself in him. That I would know if I crossed the line. How did I get so far over it?

How? I spent too many years carrying on like a man! My own distorted spin on the women's liberation and bra burning era I grew up in. The safety thing, again. As a woman, safety in a man's world required liberation from myself. What a paradox! The *inner male* I took on for strength was the one leading me astray. The very behavior I despised in a man who could not honor, recognize, or value a woman was the very behavior I supported when my male side shadowed my female side. Funny. Just had a flash of chasing my shadow when I was a kid. When I let "him" lead, I'm chasing my shadow, going nowhere fast.

Did I lose myself in what I felt driven to, or find myself? God, I'm glad I hit the wall before all this happened. I don't regret for a minute letting the woman in me take the lead these past few years. I don't regret the time I've taken to get to know her, to learn to trust her. She has the map to my psyche. The wisdom and strength I need to hold true to my soul's calling. And, through all of this, she is showing me how to give *of* myself without giving *up* myself. Better for my inner male to provide the fuel and momentum under *her* direction and inspiration. That way they *both* arrive at a place they actually want to be. A much healthier arrangement!

JOURNAL • Thursday, 2:00 p.m., June 2

If I really value myself, where is the mirror that validates it?

Just look around at the people in your life who reflect to you love. There are many.

Yes, but when I look around for a special significant-other-male to reflect love, I see no one. Am I that off base? It's all so odd.

And, why am I still here in this showroom? What I could have done with this place! After a year, my suggestions continue to be overlooked and rendered impotent. Joel says he respects my opinions, but then he gets caught up in his own power and control games. Where do I go from here? This place has no creative outlet for me. Only chaos and confusion, and God knows I've had enough of that in my other jobs. I don't want this kind of stuff anymore. Surely there is something I can do that would peak my interest and pay my bills without prostituting or compromising my talents.

FUNNY TIMING • IN THE MARGINS

Went to a gallery opening on Saturday night with Emily. Wine and hors d'oeuvres. That was fun. The Course group and brunch took up the better portion of Sunday morning and early afternoon. Felt a little antsy Sunday night, so headed out to hang at the bookstore for a while. Bought a book on tantric sex. If I can't do it, at least I can read about it! Maybe it will answer some of these questions I have about passion. Eric called while I was out. Funny timing. He's been on my mind but I've been afraid to talk to him since "that night." Returned his call but got his machine. This is so weird. I vacillate from fantasizing about him, to aching for Ray, to being pissed off at them both. Am I sick or what?

And if that's not enough, Samantha's friend Barry called. She is really wanting us to meet. He knows my situation and has just gotten out of a long-term relationship as well, so neither one of us is jumping in. He is probably doing this to get Sam off his back! Have my reservations about this. Things are complicated enough, but I want to be open to new experiences. What have I got to lose? I will look at it as an adventure. If I don't like him – or he me – fine. Sam will be satisfied that we followed through, and that will be the end of it.

CONTEMPLATIVE MEDITATION
Monday, June 6

- *Passion:* Passion *chosen* is empowering, even with its vulnerabilities and risks. Passion *not chosen*, experienced through insane out-of-control moments, is debilitating.
- *Expression of passion chosen:* I claim my power and extend. I respond to something deep within. When I *choose* passion, I allow it to channel *through* me. I see my *choice* as contributing to the "cause" of my experience.
- *"Insane" passion:* I give my power away. I react to something or someone outside myself. With no choice, I am a slave to circumstances. I see *effects* as contributing to the "cause" of my experience.

- ***Passion's yardstick:*** How do I feel? Insane passion is addictive. Complete with emotional hangover. Its fix is short lived. Passion chosen is expansive. Sustaining. There is no hangover.
- ***Cause and Effect:*** There is a key here in how we create, or should I say co-create, our reality – in whether our passion expands or devours. Do I see cause, then effect? Or effect, then cause? Where do I see cause in my life? Do I see God as Cause or outside circumstances as cause? If I see outside circumstances as cause, then I am saying effect creates cause. Now creation is upside down. The world – my world – becomes chaos. I've taken power from God and given it to circumstances, and if I do that, I too have lost power.

Holy shit. Enough, Bernadette! Play with it. Don't get anal. Guess I'll just contemplate this *lightly*.

SPIRIT DIALOG • Wednesday, 11:31 p.m., June 8

Today was Ray's birthday and I did not call him.

Found myself wondering what he did and if anyone we know acknowledged it. Felt strange and sad not to celebrate this day with him. Really hurt. I wanted to rake him over the coals for putting us in this position, where I couldn't feel free to wish him a happy birthday.

I got him a card, anyway. Guess I won't be sending it. I drew a Rune about calling him tonight. Got *Standstill.*[*] Guess I won't be calling him either.

Bernadette, everything that happens is in your best interest. Listen to the Runes. They will tell you true because you trust them. Ray's voice sounded strained, on Lea's answering machine this afternoon, because he was feeling a sense of loneliness and

---

[*]Ralph Blum, *The Book of Runes* (New York, 1987, Oracle Books / St. Martin's Press)

accountability on his birthday. Measuring himself, to some degree, at a point yet unconscious.

Your silence to him speaks more loudly than all that you would scream at him now. It is so unlike the Bernadette he thinks he knows.

Do not give Eric airs or put him on a pedestal. You will challenge him, as you will any man you choose to be involved with. You can do no less, as this passion you have will seek expression. The door cannot be closed, so go with the flow. It is the only real choice that you can make.

Do not berate yourself your imaginings, as they are creating a future for you. You will have a forum for your passion and your art will attest to that passion in Truth.

Ask for what you want, but ask intelligently!

JOURNAL • Thursday, June 9

The fool didn't know what he had when he had it! Hell, I didn't know what I had when I handed it over to him! This is about my knowing what I have and placing my own value on it. Not asking him, or any other man, what "it" is worth!

DINNER DATE • IN THE MARGINS

Ray has asked me out for dinner next Tuesday. June the fourteenth. Our anniversary and my cut off date for a decision. Is this the sign that I have been asking for? I'm not sure how to take this. He didn't mention the date *or* our anniversary. I wonder what he is thinking. Asked him about his birthday. Guess no one acknowledged it. Just his Mom. I felt sad.

SPIRIT DIALOG • Thursday

Release that which you would project about dinner with Ray. You do not know what would be on the screen. Let go the images and let the Holy Spirit run the projector on Tuesday, not before.

You do not know where Eric is in relating to you, or why he does not call you back. You project rejection, charity, just another "asshole" man. Let go the images. You are transferring from Ray to Eric. Ray is no longer worthy of your guilt. He is not what you thought; so, now you see Eric this way. Sensitive, communicative, feeling, responsible. He is worthy, so you transfer guilt. Actually, you divide guilt between the two men.

Do you not see what it is you are doing? You must first make your victims worthy, for you believe the magnitude of your guilt is that great. And yet it is nothing! The screen is white. The film has not yet run. Stop projecting for either man. You know nothing of any of this! Nothing.

Cease the ego meanderings and turn them over to me. As long as you can only relate to a screen, let me run the film. Shall we not try something different? Even your happiest images lead you to sadness and seeming loss. And yet, the screen is your own creation by which you are so mesmerized you can no longer tell the real from the false. You are lost in the screen. Let me use it to help us both.

Now, reread this and go about your day. Do not forget. Let go the images. Allow me to direct for you. I understand that all you can do here is project, but your film is stuck. Let's see if we can't bring in something different for you to view.

You are neither alone nor without comfort, though as you feel your passion in the form of rage you are blind to the light. Ego will always take your passion and twist its intent. See anger, see lust as but splinters of something far greater. Far holier. You are gaining an understanding of this through your cause and effect contemplations. Keep those in mind.

Light Child. Peace Child.

Wow. That writing felt different. Is *me* who I think?

JOURNAL • Friday, June 10

My distorted twist on security and faithfulness. As long as Ray needed me, he would never leave. His right brain, artistic self *needed* my left brain, take care of the details self. He could be the visionary while I balanced the checkbook. Security perfected, as long as he stayed on his side of the fence. When he didn't, I had to protect my territory. Do more. Control more. Know more. Prove to him why he did not want to – or worse yet, why he couldn't.

In the years he was hiding his drinking, this pattern worked well for both of us. He could drink and not worry about getting caught tripping over the details. As long as I took care of business, he had his cover. When he drank, he was *dependent* on me – I was *secure* – and we were *faithful* to each other in maintaining this unspoken contract. Though I didn't create his dependency, I acquiesced to it because it so perfectly answered to my need for security.

God, no wonder those first years of sobriety were so rough. He was coming to. Releasing his dependency. Claiming his responsibilities. I didn't know how to be in this new relationship. I had no value if he didn't need me. I was in a foreign land with the wrong currency. We both were.

Damn. I didn't want to be the one worrying about the details of living. I wanted him to take an interest and relieve me of my duties, but when he did my reaction was knee-jerk-stupid. Protect. Defend. Justify.

The resentments were blinding, exhausting. And yet, I couldn't leave him. I couldn't handle the guilt that came with the thought. So, I stayed. And now I look like the faithful one and he the guilty deserter. What a mess. What a joke.

RACING HORMONES • JOURNAL
Saturday, June 11

Numb again. My fantasy world is definitely better than what actually goes on. I guess that's why they call it fantasy.

Eric just dropped me off. Spent the afternoon at the theater. Sharing that time with him brought home the realization that he is a better friend than my current physical needs will allow me to appreciate. I feel such a strong attraction to him right now. Guess this is what they call rebound, or transference. I have to be careful. My twisted mind goes straight to being afraid of what Ray may have told Eric about our sex life, about his lost desire for me. And that slams me right into my "I am flawed not enough for any man" wall. I know it's an absurd waste of energy to even venture an inquiry from that space and defend my case, but ego will not let me rest with this. It is screaming, "You idiot! Eric wouldn't *want* to make love to you because Ray has told him your secret. You're flawed!"

Hell, that hasn't even remotely come up. What an imagination! We are not acting as anything more than the good friends we've been for all these years. We haven't even mentioned the kiss! And yet, I can't help wondering if I should feel humiliated when I spend time with him, though he says he identifies more with me than Ray. Damn these racing hormones and insecurities. The kiss between us was my choice, my kiss, and Eric was kind. That's all there was to it.

I need to follow Sandra's suggestion. If I want to create a new reality with a man, if I want to imagine a lover, he needs to be faceless in my fantasies. I lose my grip on reality when I use a familiar form. Eric is a good friend and my fantasy world could jeopardize or, at the very least, complicate the hell out of our friendship. And *that* we don't need.

I know he's still sorting through his feelings toward the gal he got involved with after he and Marsha separated. How coincidentally odd that he spent time with her last night! That had to leave him with a hell of a residual to work through this afternoon. His distraction was evident the minute I got into his car. He's not been entirely open with me and I can only guess at why. The last thing he needs is a rebounding friend whose husband calls him regularly!

I want to cry but the tears won't come. I'm frustrated as hell and tired of hurting. I'm craving romantic, passionate, male attention. Maybe I was hoping Eric and I could add that dimension to our relationship because I thought it would feel safe, since we've been friends for so long. A compromise? Again, my fantasies. How do I create a new life without them?

On an afternoon like this how do I live with them? It's only 5:00 and the night ahead looks very long and entirely different from what I had planned. Ironic that he gave me a pep talk about how I shouldn't be afraid to ask for what I want. Told me about this gal who called to ask him out. It didn't feel appropriate to take his advice and express *to* him my desire *for* him. I didn't want to put him in the awkward position of having to say, "You're a good friend, but . . ." And honestly, I could not go through another rejection.

Couldn't someone pursue me, just until I get my confidence up? Where do I find this guy? How do I meet him?

Seems Ray is experiencing a similar dilemma since he and Shelly broke up. Ray called and asked Eric how and where he meets women. That part didn't disturb me as much as finding out that he'd told Eric he asked me out to dinner for – in Ray's words – our anniversary. Our anniversary? News to me! Eric questioned Ray about his motives, about sending mixed signals. He asked me why I was going. If I thought I would take Ray back. Is this another sign? Eric didn't have to say anything about Ray or their conversation – or put me on the spot about my feelings. I wonder if this *anniversary* dinner is going to be a mistake. Looks like June the fourteenth really could turn out to be a decision making day. I have to prepare.

God, I know that everything happens in divine order but when does the fun start? I feel like I am just barely hanging onto the outermost fringes of a life. I'm a woman who has needs and feelings, and I've done without for a lot longer than the four months this separation presents. Please, help me with this. Now!

PREPARATION • JOURNAL • Sunday, June 12

Been doing a lot of thinking and I need to take notes on some of the things I want to say to Ray after dinner Tuesday. It's important I get these thoughts organized, so I don't back down. Here goes.

• Ray, you asked why I put the photo of me (from our honeymoon) on the fridge? Because, even as screwed up as that Bernadette was, she had something that I've lost. In all her craziness, she still *owned* her sexuality. She owned her passion. She owned her creativity. She owned her capacity for pleasure. And she was still willing to risk their expression in the pursuit of love. She is up there to remind me that I can know that again.

• In trying to be the good wife, I lost her essence. I let society, and you, set the standard. Who is Mrs. Raymond Smith anyway? That's not who I am. That's a shell I took on. You not only got to keep your identity when we got married, you got to add mine to it. Mrs. Fairy Tale Wife subordinates needs for self to husband. I thought if being your wife wasn't fulfilling to me, it must be my fault. I stood corrected and apologetic for my needs. Guilty for trying to regain the woman, the sensuality, I'd lost.

• I was slowly, insidiously put in my place by your lack of response. You never beat me down with it. You just didn't respond. That's abuse. And I, the good wife, adjusted to fit the circumstances as they presented themselves, business or personal. My needs as a woman, my needs as an artist, all became secondary to yours. Hell, even my artistic creations came to revolve around the needs of your business ventures.

• You get to run around out there now, with your sexuality intact, just like you did before we married. But who am I now? The *shell* that got left behind, trying to scramble for an identity other than the cast off wife? I want my sexuality back. Dammit, you are not carrying it with you while you run around doing the same old shit! There *is* no Mrs. Smith.

You don't own that and you don't own her. And you do not get to conveniently overlook what was given to you to honor and cherish. I am taking it all back. My sexuality and my identity. Who I was before I gave it all to you. I do not have to reconcile myself to you. I do not have to keep the doors open. I do not have to fix it. If I have to file for divorce to claim me, I will.

ANNIVERSARY • JOURNAL • Tuesday, June 14

Today would have been our nineteenth anniversary. We're not divorced, so I guess it still is. Certainly, it's not the celebration I would have hoped for.

Tonight, Ray takes me out for dinner and hasn't the slightest idea what has been going on inside me. I feel so sad now. Like I did when all this started. So much time, so much energy, so many dreams. It's hard to fathom that this could really be the end. The purpose of it all. To come to this place in order to begin a new life without each other.

I hate that I lost myself in the marriage. I hate that I couldn't see what was happening while it was happening, so I could have challenged it more intelligently, instead of wasting energy on petty battles. It might have saved us. But then maybe not. Maybe we weren't to be saved.

God, I want to run out of this showroom. It's hard being here today. I am grieving for what could have been. I thought being the best wife I could be would be fulfilling to me and satisfying to us both. Instead, I created a monster that neither of us cared for. What a joke!

What is my intention for this evening? To find the Bernadette I lost. The Bernadette who is just herself, and wife to no man. I want to be free to express, to feel, to know myself as a woman, as an artist – without the roles or the rules.

God, I'm scared. I know what I need to do tonight but I don't want to hurt him, or myself, in going through this process. The caretaker in me wants to protect him. The woman in me wants out of her restraints and has no idea how she *really* feels about this man.

It's uncanny how most of the tarot cards I have drawn lately focus on the story of Eros and Psyche. Psyche, casting the light on her beloved – betrayal – loss – grief – resolve and dedication – purpose and patience – going into the depths of the underworld, a seemingly impossible trek to survive. Each step's challenge, parallel to my own. Guess that's why I've always loved this mythological set.[*] The stories are awesome in how they speak to me. The cards I pulled for this evening's dinner with Ray talked of re-union, recommitment, celebration. How odd! My plan for tonight – this divorce "emancipation" proclamation – seems contrary to the cards. Like I am shutting the door for good on any possibility of reconciliation.

Feeling just a little guilty about letting him buy me dinner, knowing what I'm going to say afterward. I can't really blame him for using Shelly as an out. It was an easier way. I mean, what if there were another man in my life, right now? Wouldn't that make tonight's task easier? Maybe. But then my motives wouldn't be clear. My intentions for myself, not pure.

This is so sad. I don't believe Ray and I can even be friends right now, and I think he feels that we can. I'm really torn. But it hurts too much to be casual, in that way, after what we've had – or what I thought we had.

Holy Spirit, You know what You're doing. I pray for the best for all concerned and for all who feel invested in this. I pray for peace. Help me.

IN THE MARGINS

I did it. And I did a damn good job. I was calm. Composed. Detached. Didn't attack him. Didn't hold anything back. I looked good. (Sounds superficial, with all the

[*]Juliet Sharman-Burke and Liz Greene, *The Mythic Tarot* (New York, 1986, Simon & Schuster)

other issues at hand, but it was important that I not look like a victim.) I felt good. I was glowing! He even commented on how green my eyes were. Startled me a little. I wonder if they changed color or if the light was playing tricks.

He took it well, I think. He didn't fight me or try to defend his position. He listened and he heard. When I finished, he shared some things with me. Things I hadn't counted on hearing, really. His words hurt, but more in the way the truth hurts when one is not ready to hear it. I didn't detect any attack or manipulation. He was sharing to come clean. No more secrets. Better to get it all out so we can deal with it. Damn.

It's going to take me some time to digest the evening.

JOURNAL • Friday, 3:30 p.m., June 17

Dear Holy Spirit, what Ray admitted to me Tuesday night is sinking in and I am desperately trying to process it. I'm looking at a betrayal that I had not anticipated. And it has nothing to do with Shelly before, during, or after.

It's hard to absorb that Ray had been looking for reasons to leave all along. That he would think I'd object to his decision to go back into acting, and then plan on using my objection as justification to leave tells me he hadn't *seen me* for a very long time. It hurts to think how much he had to withdraw emotionally to buy into that idea as even a remote possibility. What a setback – and surprise – it must have been for him when I supported his decision. His dream. Damn. This hurts!

Why feel so alone and sad *now*? I should have felt it then. Maybe I did. Maybe that's why the chronic fatigue.

A deep chill is setting in as I write this. My God. No wonder our business ventures were always a struggle. He embraced them as ways to pay me off and get out. All the time, talent, and energy I put in that he *accepted*, knowing what he intended! I used to feel like we were just unlucky, but now I see the universe was kind by not granting us the success we hoped for. There is a justice present.

Who is this man? Was any love or support between us real? How do I find peace with this?

JOURNAL • Saturday, 12:00 p.m., June 18

Just finished talking with Sandra. Re-affirm! Love *is* real. Ray and I *do* share love. The tenderness expressed, in years gone by, was real. Perhaps Ray wasn't so depressed as he was *grieving* our relationship, as I am now. I need to watch out for ego chatter that tries to discredit everything we shared, still share at a higher level. All is as planned. I will pray for assistance, humility, and forgiveness.

IN THE MARGINS

Ray, how could you watch me die and never say a word to anyone? Why didn't you help me, when you saw me trying to get the spark back, instead of plotting your departure? You were throwing dirt on me but I wasn't dead! You buried me alive and left me to dig myself out.

JOURNAL • Sunday, June 19

God, I'm depressed. Here I am, busy with all these extra curricular activities: looking for ways to revive my art, possibly changing jobs – but no Ray to share with. I miss him. It feels like he should be pulling up the driveway any minute now. Like he should be coming home! He would have really enjoyed last night. Carousing in the Highlands with Paul and his friend. Well, maybe not with me, huh?

I insist that he consider us divorced and now I'm grieving *us* more than ever. So, where are all the guys who could distract me, now that I'm available? They're out to lunch. I'm just *friend* material to them – a buddy to chum around with. What a mess I am!

Well, now I've complicated my evening. Paged Ray. What if he doesn't call back? What if he does? Can't undo the page. God, the silence is deafening. Should I spout off more of my thoughts about the betrayal or just tell him "never mind" and hang up? If the outcome is assured, as Spirit says, why can't I just let go and rebuild my life?

JOURNAL • Monday, June 20

Talking with Ray last night helped me see how many of the feelings fueling the letter I wrote to the Holy Spirit on Friday were coming from my old negative core. It's just not that simple! What he shared Tuesday night was for healing – to come clean – not for validating worn-out "I'm not worthy therefore Ray's attitude proves it" punishment stuff.

Good Lord, does the ego chatter ever stop? Even when I think I am being profoundly clear in my insights, I find I'm only dipping back into the toilet. Back into the same old shit!

JOURNAL • Tuesday, June 21

Wow! I'm writing this in the clinic lobby while Ray is in session with Sandra. I can't believe we drove out here together! Even with separate sessions, this is still phenomenal.

Holy Spirit, do your work. I will try to be patient. Help me to hear you. I pray that Ray may hear you as well. Open your heart, Ray.

Prayer (while waiting for my session)
My brother is not here to attack me.
He is here to love me. He *is* loving me.
Ray is not here to attack me. Ray is here to love me.
Ray *is* loving me.
I am not here to attack Ray. I am here to love Ray.
I *am* loving Ray.
Sandra is not here to attack us.
Sandra is here to love us. Sandra *is* loving us.
Love is real.

EXPECTATIONS • IN THE MARGINS

The ride back from our sessions with Sandra was quiet. I have to be careful about the expectations I want to attach to this carpooling episode. I have to be patient and let it be. God, help me.

JOURNAL • Wednesday, June 22

Not a bad morning in the showroom. Managed to lose my thoughts in the busywork, but this afternoon I'm again wondering about Ray. Why can't I let go of the feeling that we belong together? It's hard for me to fathom how Ray can be so out of touch with us. Does he still believe himself to be in love with Shelly? Does he really believe he does not, cannot, never did, love me?

If this is going to take much longer, send me someone to spend time with. Am I to know myself as this new woman – in a vacuum? Hell, it's all theory so far. How about some practice?

God, was I that far off with Eric? And Sam's friend Barry getting sick just before our blind date is too bizarre. Are You saving me? For what? For Ray? Is this some kind of joke? Is there something more I'm supposed to do to help him? I can't believe You would make me responsible for that. That's skirting too close to manipulation stuff.

God, I don't even know if I like Ray right now. He's so self-absorbed. I want some *positive* male attention. To have fun and get reacquainted with my passion for life.

How about a sign? A heavenly nod? A phone call from Ray professing his love would be nice! Or a call from Eric for a night out? Maybe a little sex between friends? Here I am, trying to bargain!

Dammit. Look at me and the work I've done. The progress I've made. It's amazing! I'm a phenomenal woman. Can no man see that? Are they not interested in phenomenal? The women in my life know. They see. Can't Ray see how lucky he is? I could be dumping on him, in rage!

Instead, he gets thought-provoking reflections of growth that give him an opportunity to grow in his response. Can't he see the value in that? I could be handling this like a Shelly. God help him then!

Wake up Ray! What are you doing?

SPIRIT DIALOG • Wednesday Evening, June 22

What information will you give me regarding Ray and myself? Are we getting back together in *this* lifetime? And what about these other men?

There have been some readjustments made regarding Eric, since last you pulled the Runes. You were too willing to move too fast. This silence, as you call it, is for Ray to catch up. Too lengthy a time with Eric, or any other for that matter, would only serve to confuse you. If you do go to bed with Eric, it will now be a choice based on something more real. We had to give you time to take him off the pedestal. Now that you see where his growth is not, you may decide against going through that door, or at least proceed with eyes open. The reemergence of his ex-girlfriend, and her timing, was no coincidence.

Your love for Ray holds true, and his for you will awaken soon. He does hold it now, but does not recognize its sincerity and importance to his soul. He will want you in a way he has never before, but give us time. We know how hard this is for you and we are doing all that should be done. You do not need the signs like you think. Are you not making it now?

Come on, guys. This hurts too bad.
Can't you do something?

We can do any number of things, but we all want what is in your best interest. Some of these things, and the timing wherewith, are not good for you or Ray!

It is time to sleep. We will write more later.
Light and Love, Child.

SPIRIT DIALOG • Thursday Evening, June 23

Okay guys, give me more stuff. Is there anything I can do to help Ray? What purpose is this time serving? Is he really doing anything, or just in denial? Tell me truly.

You must see for Ray. See him awakening. Do not hold the vision of him as hopeless or helpless for, in Truth, he is not lost. And in Truth he is truly.

You have fallen away from your morning meditation. Get back to it. It was part of the acceleration before and can be so again. Now is the time to get back. These other men would divert your energies, and Ray needs your attention. He is stuck and this was a risk. Know your connection and allow your Highest Self to touch him in heart. Remember how you saw yourself in his heart this morning. Continue to do so. It is very powerful, the stirrings.

Do not give up on him, as you did not want him to give up on you. Who would betray whom by giving up? Heed your own words, Sunday evening, and do not do the same to him. See him total. Feel him total. Bless him fully and you will know your Father's Love. You must do the work. Ray is counting on you to remember who he is. A miracle takes but an instant, and in that instant time is erased. Now visualize and rest in peace.

Love and Light.

JOURNAL • Thursday Evening

Fears, regarding Ray, that are making me uncomfortable.

- That he is still trying to make it work with Shelly. That he will enlist his talent for control and manipulation to win her back.
  (my unworthiness stuff)
- That he is cut off from feelings for me as a woman for whom he could feel passion.
  (more unworthiness stuff)

- That he will never see me for who I am, but forever "frozen in time" for who I was. Natalie says it's his own guilt that is frozen and projected onto me, but knowing that isn't always a comfort.
(my punishment stuff)
- That he has wasted valuable time in not keeping up his appointments with Sandra. Where would we be now if he had been seeing her all along?
(my judgment stuff)
- That he still doesn't get it and never will. I'll be lost forever loving someone who doesn't love me.
(my punishment stuff)

SPIRIT DIALOG • Friday, June 24

I can't shake the feeling that Ray went out on a date tonight. Okay, I have to focus. Sandra wants me to open a dialog with you guys on her behalf. I don't know why she thinks I can do this. It really pushes me to another level of intimidation with this whole writing process. Maybe I'm afraid because I still wonder if I'm not making up all this. And yet, you guys were right on the mark with Shelly: the breakdown, the flowers, even their plans to move in together. So, I will try not to question or censor what I write tonight. I haven't the foggiest idea what Sandra's issue is. This really challenges me.

Any information you give will be appreciated. Thank you.

The next few weeks will be a blessing for you, with all there is to do. It will also give you reason not to call Ray, and he will start to wonder where you are. Offer to split your Tuesday session with him. Another boost from Sandra will not hurt. You are clearing the path to him in heart, once again in your meditations.

You worry that Ray will file bankruptcy unnecessarily but consider that perhaps he needs to do so to clear out all the old energy. His debts are representative of his guilt for self and lack of forgiveness for a past of which he is not proud. You will be taken care of. You have no need to file bankruptcy.

You may have lost self to him, in the form of your perception as wife, but you did not lose love for him, though your love was distorted. You understood the meaning of surrender, at some levels more so than Ray was able to reach. You tried to show him and could have done so, but the bonds that tied him were stronger than you could handle. The drain on your energy was tremendous. He had to leave, to do it this way, to free himself.

The angels you saw in meditation, celebrating his return to you, are with him now as we write, and are watchful of him. Keep praying and visualizing so that he may know your love. Your heart knows he will return. He will be "unstuck" soon.

Know and accept the truth in your heart. Your path is to be together, and truly now there is more honesty between you than there has ever been. You are no longer underfoot for Ray to blame. This time is for him to see his own mirror, however long that takes, without blaming you for his current situation. You are simply not in it, except in the most positive light. Believe that what you show him is a surprise and a challenge. Be persistent and consistent in your honesty. He is starting to wonder why he is doing this. The steam is dissipating with each interaction with you. Yes, he still plays with the idea of Shelly, but you need not worry about that any more now than before. That simply is not to be. If not you, it will be no one. He will not be satisfied with anyone else, nor they with him.

You are much more flexible in your ability to love than he at this point; and so, believe it or not, you could find another to replace Ray and relate in the manner that Sandra teaches.

She teaches well, which is also why she must go through so much. Have you not benefited from her path in this lifetime? You go back very far with each other. She is as the daughter who would share the new found light with her mother, to break the ancestral ties. No more shall history bear either of you down, unless you choose to go back, which is always your prerogative, but worry not. You and Sandra have come too far and you are both working together now to keep yourselves straight. The energy exchange between you is tremendous and instantaneous. Your words are but shadows of what you truly give to each other. You are right to bless your union.

Sandra need only know that what occurs is in the requirement of a process that she has chosen. She is not without power. All that is happening will show its purpose as others cross her path. She is a selective teacher, not in that she will choose those she would teach but rather they will recognize the precise nature of what she would offer. Not many will understand but those who do, such as yourself, will count for many, for teachers of teachers must share with each other. We have known of your loneliness for a long time, for one who would challenge you truly in the way that you needed to be challenged. Fine tuning has been hard for you, in that there have not been many you could look to who were not already looking to you. Sandra's requirements, as yours, are high, but you both must also learn to lighten as you go through your process. It is not all work.

Sandra is not at the mercy of circumstance. All has been chosen. She need only to look in the mirror and accept her own light. This is not about earning love through appearance or action, but accepting love through awareness of her true nature.

JOURNAL • Saturday Evening, June 25

The following felt channeled. It came spontaneously. Spirit urged me to pick up a piece of paper and a pen, and not let these thoughts pass. I don't know what I'm to do with this except to copy it into my journal and save it.

Ray, you are out there because you have not forgiven. That you are out there is evidence of your lack of forgiveness. Were you to forgive, you would know your home and your Love which awaits your return. All this action, all these antics, would display their meaninglessness to you. That you remain out there shows that you do not yet see this.

Your use for others still is in the realm of the physical and material. Scott's purpose for you could be far greater than sales tricks. He is the one who cared for you when you were too drunk to drive yourself home, so many years ago. You are much in the same place with guilt eating away at you, as you were then, except that you are not drinking – yet. But heed that which you know. You can take this as far as you feel you need to, and you can stop at any given point. The choice is yours.

It is hard for those who love you and see, to watch you, to hear you, as you go in your circle ever so tightly. Open your heart. This is about your heart. About forgiveness that frees you to love truly. Shelly and you were but shadows mimicking love's nature. Shadows not truly your own. Will you be content with the shadows? Shall you be consumed by the darkness in which you take your strides? Can you not see the light that those who care for you would offer? Must you cheapen their support by reducing it to that which serves your material gains? Independence, this need, is of your ego.

It ended here because the phone rang.

JOURNAL • Sunday Afternoon, June 26

The following information came while getting ready for Sunday's Course group. This writing felt more like a psychic read in that I chose the words to express the information that was coming in. This could be useful to Ray if he were ready to hear. In the meantime, it's really helping me understand where I need to do my healing work. It's given me a way to go back, to uncover the guilt that got buried and examine what happened between us. (Now I know what my snow and ice dreams have been trying to tell me.) It's also given me a very different view of Divine Intervention at a time in my life when so much *appeared* to be going wrong.

- *Look for the clues*:
  That Ray would take action to contact Shelly, after all these years, *is a clue*, the *first* clue, pinpointing the time and space in which our guilt was frozen. (Thus the dreams always with snow and ice.) To heal this guilt I need to look at what was going on between *us* when they *first* met.

  What was my attitude then?
  "*I don't need you. I can make it on my own just fine.*"
  What do I perceive Ray to be reflecting to me now?
  "*I don't need you. I can make it on my own just fine!*"
  Witnessing that mirror *now*, when I am not presently feeling that way, is the *second clue*, pointing to where guilt was frozen. Both clues are indicating our need to address that point in time, before we can go forward. It is our Achilles heal.

- *See Divine Intervention*:
  That's why it had to be Shelly and not just any other woman or circumstance. She was inserted at that time by a Higher Knowing. His strong attraction to her was planted to guarantee the catalyst effect when we were ready to move into our next phase of challenged growth. We needed the additional years, after their first encounter, to strengthen the bond between us, to soften our edges. This was the period when we most strongly acted out the guilt we'd been carrying all along. When the guilt we brought into the marriage became evident. "Melting snow" revealed it. (Thus the dreams with snow and ice in various stages of thaw.) The thaw was occurring for one of us and so had to happen for both of us, revealing the guilt that was frozen at the core.

- *Negative core belief in action:*
  My "thaw" encouraged me to forgive myself, but I attempted forgiveness by "making it up" to Ray. I tried to *earn his love*, to apply forgiveness by becoming *an even better wife*. Forgiveness is not about changing or earning or making it up to someone. It is about recognizing that I am all right as I am *in Truth,* as I am in acceptance of the Whole. Believing that I had to change to forgive, or to be forgiven, froze my guilt and Ray's. Six years of correcting guilt is not forgiveness.

- *How forgiveness works:*
  Spirit says that I am Ray's partner in this because I will understand, or rather recognize, the miracle of enlightenment. I will be able to accept an acceleration, or time collapse, and will not demand lengthy proof of his sincerity, as others in more traditional time frames and concepts of the unforgivable would. I will be able to follow my heart and be strong, even though others will question my judgment.

- *Witness the miracle:*
  My offering Ray the cans of tuna from the cupboard and bread from the freezer (that had been here since he left), when I found out he was low on money and not eating, is my desire to offer a miracle. A symbolic act. In offering to Ray, I give to myself. My amusing metaphor for Christ's miracle when feeding the multitudes. Fishes and loaves? Tuna and multigrain!

- *This to Ray:*
  Change your intention for being "out there" and you will change your results. Intention to enforce and maintain separation will meet with frustration and failure. Intention to love, to show love, in order to end separation will meet with peace and success.

End of read.

JOURNAL & SPIRIT DIALOG
Sunday Evening, June 26

Some catch up.

After I saw Ray at Sandra's office Tuesday afternoon, I went into deep fatigue – falling asleep standing up! Wednesday and Thursday were awful days with much sadness – some panic and deep depression. Friday was better, but after coming home from an evening out with Barbara, I felt – feared Ray had also gone out for the evening – on a date. After talking with Ray, Saturday, about the finances and Tuesday's appointment with Sandra, he mentioned hitting the emotional skids on Wednesday and Thursday and that he'd met Scott for dinner, Friday night. Seems I empathed again. I still take on his feelings as mine without realizing it. Wow!

This afternoon, The Course gang christened Emily's deck with the Fiesta we'd been planning. Had a great time. Everyone brought a dish to pass and music to share. When Paul played *Shattered* by the Rolling Stones, I could not sit still. It was wild, dancing to *Shattered*, knowing that I wasn't but could have been. An empowering rush of defiance came up like "Hell no! Not me!" Haven't let loose like that in years. Paul and I talked about going dancing. Just to shake off the world. Just to play.

I am feeling more willingness to be playful, even with Ray. To allow him to see me at play. To me dance is play. I want to dance more. It's a great way to express, to release my passion, my anger, my lust, my sorrow.

Slipped out from the festivities for about an hour to have my first channeled session with someone Sandra knows, who lived nearby. I'd been wanting to do this for a while. Today it felt right. I need to listen to the tape to see if it recorded properly. All I can remember now is being told that Ray would be back for Christmas and that we still had much work to do. And that I would benefit from reviewing two past lives. I was given the names Francesca and Lucinda.

Spirit, I am open to whatever will assist or expedite this process with Ray. If the outcome is assured, then the outcome need not be the goal. The process, and what I learn in the process, is where I need to place my attention. Maybe I can allow myself to experience the benefits of risking vulnerability with Ray, but you need to show me when and where. So often I miss the opportunities.

And what am I supposed to do with this past life information? I'm drawing a blank.

Francesca. Lucinda. Feel the names. Are they not hot blooded? Depicting warmer temperaments?

Oh, Francesca could throw things. She had quite the temper, but she loved so deeply. Both were simple women of simple means, with deep passions. Ray knew Francesca. He was one of her lovers. Much younger than she, but one of her favorites, for he learned well. Francesca was your gypsy in spirit. She could read the cards quite well. She followed one love, though she had many lovers. Her spirit was pure and untainted. When she gave, she gave fully. You hold many of her qualities in this lifetime, in your commitment to love. But you do not take her risks.

Lucinda will show you through dance movements how to open your spirit. Dance will bring you to freedom of expression in your art.

I also want to know, what is this *"sign of fire and water"* that I keep getting? It came up in the channeled session, as well. What does it mean, or will it come to mean?

Okay, so don't tell me.

SPIRIT DIALOG • Monday, June 27

Spirit, here I go again. I'd like to access information that would be helpful to Sandra. You know I'm nervous about doing this. I will try not to censor any impressions that come. Please, help me to open so I can be of assistance to others.

And, anything that might be new, regarding Ray and myself. In this order please.

Sandra is getting ahead of herself, as the tarot card you pulled indicated. That which she fears has no form, only voice, and it is the voice of guilt and days gone by. But let her remember that her past need not predict her future. This she knows. This she must remember.

First, she worries that the well may be dry. Then she worries that she will not have the strength to carry the many full buckets from the well. From "nothing" to not knowing how to handle "too much." The well is not dry. She must remember she is not expected to make every run. Once Adam makes his adjustments, he will be more than able and willing to make the runs with her.

Remember, Sandra, this well is not yours alone but shared property. These runs can be joyous or grueling. Worry not if you or Adam spill a drop or two or, for that matter, a whole bucket. And consider this: that if you continue to look over your shoulder to monitor Adam, you most likely will be the one to trip on a rock and spill yours, as you overly concern yourself with where he may be spilling his. Even water spilled can nourish where it falls and refreshes that which would receive its blessings. The most parched and barren has a need and a life not immediately evident to the oh-so-discerning eye. So relax and enjoy the trip. A funny! End of our bucket and well story. Look to the card that Bernadette pulled for you, for the serious view.

First impressions, dear one. Learn to accept after you recognize. Not argue. Not alter. Accept. Do not fear to stop writing here. We will give you more later. Rest now. You have done well.

> *Ego will always take your passion and twist its intent. See anger, see lust as but splinters of something far greater. Far holier.*

JULY

TOADS AND PRINCES • JOURNAL • Friday, July 1

Last night's conversation with Ray was good. Actually, most of our conversing this week has been good, though tiring for me. Being this new me with him is more work than I realized. I see that Spirit knows what is best. As much as I miss him, being with him for 24/7 would leave me drained.

Today has been a strange day – with the anger that has come up toward men, and anger toward myself for the tone I set with them by always seeming to be the initiator. Ray, all through the marriage. Eric, in the friendship. Barry, with the blind date. Extra curriculars with Paul. If I am not the one doing, nothing gets done. More belief system stuff.

What is this telling me? That I am even noticing and getting angry is evidence that I'm willing to be vulnerable to seeing, to acknowledging my needs. That I'm willing to admit that I have not allowed any one male to meet these needs because I have not been willing to risk *being still* – to stop initiating long enough to see who *would* meet them. This anger is a sign of growth coming from a place that says it is time for me to change my ways. Yes, I'm vulnerable to needing interaction with – attention, validation from men. No, I don't always want to feel like I'm the one responsible for that occurring – in maintaining or saving the marriage, in maintaining or pursuing the friendships.

I would like to feel men are just as interested in relating to me, as I to them. Right or wrong, I *need* this. I need to see them take some action. I need to feel their initiative. And I'm really pissed with myself for not *being still* long enough to see how one-sided these, and other relationships with men, have been.

For example, if I had never called Eric after Ray and I split, would he have called me? Possibly not. Ego says *probably* not. That's a fearful, lonely thought. So if I call him, I don't have to face the painful truth that I'm not worthy of his attention or concern.

The women in my life know how to meet this need. How to extend themselves in a relationship. Women just seem to understand this naturally. I wonder, are men even capable? Hell, taking a little bit of initiative in relationships – say, thirty percent of the time – would be a vast improvement for them.

How far back does this pattern go for me? Dad wasn't emotionally available when I was a kid. Not in the way that I needed. There was no relating with him. I was afraid of him. With his drinking and his stresses, I didn't *want* to initiate anything with him. And I've been making up for it with every man since. Initiate. Coerce. Manipulate. Whatever it's taken to maintain a relationship. Weird twist. It might have saved me a lot of energy and heartache if I could have risked with Dad, the first significant man in my life. Even thirty percent initiative on *my* part would have been a vast improvement in that relationship. Who knows what I might have experienced. Maybe a little forgiveness, even. For both of us.

And how does this relate to God? Am I angry that I have to work so hard to find Him? Does He not notice that I am gone? Why doesn't He come get me? Doesn't He care? Am I the only one seeking this relationship?

I wonder what it would feel like to be pursued in a relationship. What my reaction would be. I can think of a few, from years ago, but they were pretty sick. And I was too needy to run in the opposite direction like I should have. Maybe I'll re-phrase that. I wonder what it would feel like to be pursued in a *healthy* relationship. Hell, then I probably would run.

I can't stand this feeling. What do I do about this? I don't know what to do about this. Has it occurred to Ray what life would be like without good old Bernadette, initiator and keeper of the relationship? I am tempted not to call Ray – or Eric – ever – just to see how long before they notice my absence.

What am I afraid of? Why does the idea of not calling – of being still – terrify me so? Why am I not willing to be vulnerable to just *being still* and seeing what or who comes to surface? God, this scares me. What if no one notices I'm gone? Then I'll know the truth, and how do I live with that? How can I *just be* if it means I'll be alone – would have *always* been alone?

What a burden *that* belief is! I am worthy of acknowledgment only if I do the work? I don't want Ray or any man to mirror that to me.

So, if I don't call, what will happen?

I must be getting at something here because I find myself entertaining suicide. Would I rather die than find out what I fear could be true? That I'm not worthy of notice? That I'm not worthy of love? That no man will ever be interested in pursuing me, in having passion, concern, love for me without my being the initiator?

Spirit, I'm scared. This anger comes from recognizing my needs and a tremendous fear that I don't deserve to have them met. And if I choose to reference God metaphorically as male, what does that tell me of my belief about God?

I don't like this feeling. I want to scream at Ray. I want him to notice that I am an important part of his life – spiritually, emotionally and physically – dammit! How can he be so casual about me? Dammit! What will it take? I feel invisible to all these men. Who is getting their attention? The Shellys in this world, that's who!

Damn, Ray. You *pursued her!* Just consider me dead! Do you feel that? Is there not a recognizable emptiness within you that says, "Bernadette is missing"?

Holy Spirit, Help me! I need to learn to forgive all these perceptions of myself, of Ray, and all the others. It just hurts. And I don't know what to do, except look "out there."

JOURNAL • Saturday, July 2

Had these thoughts as I reread yesterday's writing.

Where is my anger, really? With men? With myself? Am I angry that my initiating behavior only seems to draw out a passive response from the men in my life? That I have not trusted my feminine energy enough to *be* in it, live my life through it, and let the *real men* step forward? It's *my own* inner male who is pissing me off. He is the one initiating. The one in control. And I am sick of him. As a woman functioning through him, I have been as invisible to myself as I have been to the men in my life.

Inventory of Belief Structures and Bridges

I am not worthy of love. Therefore:
1. I cannot just "be" and be loved.
2. In relationships with men, I must do the work or "it" won't happen.
3. Men won't feel passion for me enough to desire, pursue, or miss me.
4. I cannot be authentic and be lovable – or loved.

As I wrote number four I realized that, in having always been so controlled by my fears, I don't know who my authentic self is. I have never felt safe to rock the boat with any man. With Dad, not at all. With Ray, only over petty stuff – and definitely not authentically. If I wanted love I had to mask my anger, my sadness, my vulnerability. And that mask didn't come off until just before Ray moved out. Actually, I don't know how authentic I was being, in what I chose to express, even then. I was on a reactionary roller coaster and yet, absurdly, still *measuring* myself. Not wanting to appear *as* angry or *as* crazy as I felt!

JOURNAL • Monday, July 4

Just got off the phone with Ray. He called to chat. Complained that he had a "hot spot" in his chest that shot straight through – front to back. Commented how this sensation started yesterday. Interesting. I had thought of him yesterday. The Course gang and I caught *Schindler's List* at a matinee. As the actor who played Schindler experienced his heart opening to the people around him, I kept thinking how much he looked like Ray in the film's black and white format. And now this phone call. Was Spirit tampering with my perception yesterday? Trying to tell me something? Is Ray's heart opening? Is the *heat* coming from a little heart chakra activity?

Ray said a number of things in that conversation that I should have responded to, but I was just not quick enough. I have to start being more responsive in the moment. I don't catch these opportunities to speak until long after they've passed. If I venture to bring them up in conversation afterward, it feels as if I am falling into the petty realm. Too late. Old news. So, I maintain my position and safely play the role of a good listener. This is not working. Maybe this is what these men are mirroring to me. Their passivity reflects some aspect of my own. There is something to this. I feel it.

So, I may initiate events and communication but I don't take the initiative with expressing my feelings *while the river is flowing*. It's as if I have to stop the river and then communicate. That's not total vulnerability. That's a bit like control. Sandra says I need to start asking myself, "Where is my freedom and my self expression, *now*?" A reality check brought to the forefront, in and of the moment.

SPIRIT DIALOG • Monday, 8:00 p.m.

This is the time for you to have peace, and time alone to contemplate. Get back into your books. Highlights are there to refresh you. All is not yet done. You still need to get back to your visualization. Try this for the next few weeks while the show at the Gift Mart is on. Then see what happens.

Can you not accept that you are receiving assistance? These men are passive to you because they are supposed to be, not because there is anything greatly wrong with you.

It is good that you look at this issue you call "initiating." We would call it control. You see this. It will assist you in better accessing your feminine energy.

We know you tire. Your energy is draining fast. Rest for the night. Perhaps tomorrow we will continue.

SPIRIT DIALOG • Wednesday, July 6

I'd like more information for Sandra. Whatever would be of benefit to her. Thank you.

We have not blocked you. You do not fully believe that the connection you feel, and information you gain in this manner of writing is real. More real than this world you create. We could give you specific information, and indeed have from time to time, but you fear being wrong so much so, that it is you who slams the door. Perhaps another way of clearing your mind and heart prior to, but keeping your attention focused? Give it time. It will come and, as you believe, it will come even more. So silly that you should know, and yet feel you need to learn. You know, in your heart, that this is a process of uncovering.

Now, what is it you feel regarding Sandra? You know that we have told you already, and yet you continue to question with your capacity for "logic." Indeed the work seems hard in your plane. You are so heavy there. You both must learn to lighten and, where you stand, the best way to do this is to play. Love is not a heavy thing. What you do in your search for love, and its extension, can be light as well. Remember it is in joy that you may both come to know your true creations. It is in fear that you perpetuate this illusion of lack.

Oh, we feel your anger at what you perceive to be our vagueness and yet it is you who create these specifics. These tedious details that we all have to work with because you believe it has to be so. Try play. Exercises in the form of play. Let go of the seriousness. This is not life or death, for you already have life!

Sandra is crushing Adam with her intensity. Her urgency. She tries to accomplish much in such a short period of time. Adam is intense also, but his rhythm is not hers. There is a pace that would be suitable for both of them.

The world cannot keep up with you two! Your requests, or attempts to fix everything now, can be maddening to those around you. In this sense, you are like children in tantrum, stomping your feet. If you insist on acting as such, perhaps you might attempt to incorporate a child's playful spirit as well?

When Ray gets through this time, he and Adam could be a support for each other. Perhaps assisting each other in absorbing the energies you both send in their direction! Reaching out the way you do is not always their first thought. They seek in their solitude. You and Sandra will not be successful in pushing these men, which is good, for as you believe you pace them, they are necessary to pace you. You cannot absorb, all at once, as much as you think you can.

A phone call from my Mom broke the writing off here.

LOVE HER, LOVE HIM • SPIRIT DIALOG
Thursday, 8:30 p.m., July 7

In meditation, I received the analogy of having an infected wound. Would I hate myself for the oozing that occurs while draining the wound – before medication can help or healing can take place? No. I recognize it as a necessary part of the healing process. I do not invest in hating myself for having an infection.

Flashback to Covington, standing in the kitchen behind the sick young woman that was me. That time was the oozing stage of a healing process. A period when the infection had to be drained before the medicine could work. Why would I hate or judge her?

For revealing her infection? And so, should forgiveness be so difficult for either Ray or Bernadette? The poison had to come out. All that was being displayed was that, and nothing more. Simply some oozing – infection – coming out, as a wound or a pimple. That is not a condemnable offense, but you have turned it into one.

Forgive what was never done to you! It was part of the natural course. Ray will see this also, and you will rejoice that you have joined together in each phase of your healing, even then. You felt, still feel, unsafe and exposed for that time period, and yet you could not have been safer. You were there this morning, were you not? Saw you not how the presence you felt over your shoulder, at that time, was an aspect of yourself – as you stand now? You were there to bless and to increase the bond you share with Ray that has always been. Know that now. Ray was with you this morning. Your awareness is his as well. We know this seems a lonely walk, but you are making tremendous strides. It is about realizing the need to forgive something that required not forgiveness to begin with, but only your perception of a need to judge that time. And now you see it was merely a pimple needed to pop for both of you.

Your Father does pursue you. The answer was given the moment you believed you separated. This you know. This you study. That is not passive and uncaring. You are pursued. Watched. Guided. Protected. Loved. All these things. You need only to accept that this is so. Can you not see that you wear blinders to this? Merely your perception.

Take this to heart throughout the day. Love her. Love him. You have your answer. You have only to cruise before you join once again, in joy, with your Beloved.

JOURNAL • Saturday, 8:51 p.m., July 9

Ray called this morning, as I was going into meditation. He wanted to know about the job interview I have coming up: what this new position would entail. Also asked if Joel was still thinking about closing the showroom and how my car was running. Said he was in a rush. Didn't want to be late for work.

Hell, he could have called this evening. It would have been more convenient for him. I know he really hates this job, though he hasn't said it. Selling cars has to be tough. Especially, if you don't have the temperament for it. So, given the stress of the circumstances, why did he *really* call this morning? Maybe he wanted to start out his day with me but didn't know how to say it, so he had to manufacture reasons like new jobs and old cars. Or was he trying to tap into my meditation time, without a conscious awareness of what the real need for contact was? Odd.

He said something about wanting to catch up with Joel. That he'd been on his mind, but wouldn't say why. I wonder if Ray is thinking about getting back into the giftware business. Maybe he wants to talk with Joel about a way to keep the showroom open. Or, maybe he wants to sell him a car! I told him that Joel basically thought he was a jerk and probably wouldn't take anything he had to say very seriously. Just rolled off my tongue like I was talking about the weather! Couldn't believe it. I didn't mean it vindictively. I was trying to spare him some embarrassment. No telling what Joel might say with what he knows about our separation. I felt like he would be gunning for Ray, but I didn't mean to put it in those terms or have it come out so bluntly. After we hung-up, I thought about calling him back and apologizing for my choice of words. Good Lord, is this what I can look forward to as I become more unrehearsed in my communication? I'm apt to say anything!

I decided not to call him – in support of the vulnerability work I've been doing – in support of allowing myself to be present to whatever my "in the moment not trying to control the river" comments might be. I have to let go and trust. But God – I still can't believe I said that!

"Gee, Ray, Joel basically thinks you're a jerk!" Ouch!

On the subject of healthy spontaneity, I've decided to take an acting class even though it scares me. I'm hoping it will blow me through this limbo I'm in with my art – if I do something creative but absolutely foreign. Something with no performance expectations attached. Talked with Ray's acting coach about taking one of his classes. Wasn't sure if I'd be welcome, since he is also Ray's friend – and his classes are for professional actors. Josh understood where I was coming from and we agreed on which class would best suit my goal.

The conversation got a little strained when Josh referred to Ray as a "fucking granite block." I know he was venting his disappointment, as a friend, because Ray didn't confide in him about what had been going on in the marriage and in his decision to step away from acting, but it really hurt to hear him say that. God, this gets difficult. I don't know what to say – or to whom.

Ray, where is your heart? When will you open your heart?

ASK HIM OUT • IN THE MARGINS

Lea saw *Forrest Gump* this week. Said it was a great movie. She is on this kick about Ray and me seeing it together. Thinks it would be good for us and that I should ask him to join me this weekend. Will have to let that one sink in a little. Not sure if I'm ready to be *that* vulnerable. Maybe she knows something I don't.

JOURNAL • Friday, July 15

The women's gathering at Lea's was quite an experience last night. When we held hands in meditation – with Sandra to my left, her hand on top – my hand felt as though it lifted up and through hers. And my physical reaction to the energy they sent me was quite a surprise. Felt like I was going to pass out and leave my body in a lump on the floor. We finished the evening with a prayer for healing and included Ray in our intentions. His calls to *both* Sandra and me first thing this morning would seem to affirm that our prayer hit its mark.

Last night, I also had a dream about Ray. I remember kissing his eyelids, his forehead, his cheeks in an attempt to awaken his passion for making love to me – and how non-responsive he was. While doing this, I heard a voice say that I needed to back off. That I was trying too hard. That it should not be work. In the dream, Ray kept talking about where we might go to eat, oblivious to the fact that I wanted to make love. Not ignoring. Not rejecting. Just not noticing.

Does this dream mean that he is not ready? His focus on where we would eat could mean he still needs to nourish himself before he can express love. The impression in the dream was that we would make love *after* we ate.

Sandra and Lea were in the dream also. The four of us started looking for a place to eat. We wandered into a tunnel and followed some train tracks that were no longer in use. They led us deep underground to a restaurant that felt like a temple. Murals of Greek architectural ruins graced the rock walls. I awoke just as we were ordering our meal.

I'm starting to get butterflies. Followed up on Lea's suggestion and asked Ray out. He hasn't seen *Forrest Gump* yet. We're going tomorrow night, and this feels just like a first date – only worse because I'm going into it with eyes wide open to all our challenges.

I am really nervous. What to say? How to act? My comment on the phone about it being good to hear his voice this morning, that met with his remark about being told he should go into voice-over work, makes me wonder if I should just slap him and cancel the whole thing. It was such an absurdly self-absorbed response. Was it just a nervous blurt on his part? One of those dumb first date remarks? I had to laugh and shake my head as I hung up the phone. Do I really want to go out with this man?

God, I don't know how to do any of this.

TIME TRAVEL • IN THE MARGINS

Natalie loaned me a book called *Awaken from the Dream*. There was a quote in it that intrigued me and, in an odd sort of way, gave me comfort with this separation from Ray.

"It was the very opposition to the thought of making a substitute for Heaven that solidified that thought and gave it its seeming reality."[*]

Kind of a take-off on "resist not evil." I make real that which I resist. I give it life because I think I have to fight it – correct it – whatever. Like in the horror flicks where the apparitions only gain strength in feeding off the fear of the victim. When I don't resist what this separation *seems* to bring, I get to see what is really here. Or something like that.

I dowsed in The Course and these two lines jumped out. They seem to help, as well.

"If it has been projected beyond your mind, you think of it as time. The nearer it is brought to where it is, the more you think of it in terms of space."

"All of time is but the mad belief that what is over is still here and now."[*]

I remember, during the show last February in New York when this separation pushed into my "space," having the uncanny feeling that if I went down to the old neighborhood where we lived when we first got married, I could literally pass myself on the street as that twenty-one year old. Like, there would be a *wrinkle in time* in which I could witness myself and it would mean being given the choice to start over. To do something differently with my life or with my marriage. It was the eeriest feeling. Wanted to go, just to see – but couldn't break away. It didn't make sense then, but it does now. These quotes somehow tie into that New York experience.

---

[*]Gloria Wapnick and Kenneth Wapnick, Ph.D., *Awaken from the Dream* (Temecula, CA, 1987, Foundation for A Course in Miracles)

[*]*A Course in Miracles* (Temecula, CA, 1985, Foundation for *A Course in Miracles*)

When all this began, I asked for help and Spirit wrote, "Time is not." I didn't understand. It pissed me off. I felt it wasn't useful information. Too cryptic for a woman whose husband just left her. Now I'm grateful. In this I'm finding peace.

Another from The Course: "When you made visible what is not true, what is true became invisible to you."

Amen to that!

SPIRIT DIALOG • Saturday, 6:15 a.m., July 16

What information can you give me about tonight's date with Ray? I welcome anything on Sandra as well. And what is this stuff that came up in the women's gathering about my being an intuitive healer? I'm having a hard time with that.

We have been giving you information all along. We speak to you even without apparent invitation. You are absorbing the information well. These are the glasses through which you must look and view all of tonight with Ray. It will help you in your search for peace. You can see that you must wholly forgive Ray. Any part that you would choose to hold back will manifest as yet another experience to work through and we know you tire of that.

The strange feeling you have, that you describe as anti-climatic, is ego's way of determining reaction to the knowledge you have of Ray's return. You think it is over and indeed it is. It all is! You are getting in touch with this through this one perceived incident which, only a few short months ago, you would have placed monumental importance on because you saw it as a future event for which to strive. Odd that it still be a future event, in your vantage point of time, and yet you have lost your investment already?

The outcome is assured and you now believe. And so ego has no place to go with this. It is done, and you experience a collapsing of past, present, and future. You see the investment of ego in time and events. Do not worry that you will be bored knowing your future. Ego is much like your soap operas that hook you into coming back to view what the ending will be, except that they never end and you just keep coming back. Time is so necessary a sleight of hand trick for ego's survival. You will not be bored but be at peace. Ego will be bored, and won't that be interesting to witness!

Your spirit could have left the body the other night at the women's gathering but you "clamped down" to contain it. You had chosen the path through the crown chakra. It would have been quite pleasant. Your concern for your friends was merely a mask, an excuse to stay in the body because of your fear. Your attempt to control. You now experience the backlash of that decision. Do not worry about your stiff neck. You have chosen this, to make you question the event rather than take for granted your first perception. You were trying to consciously be aware of leaving your body through the evening, though you are also not aware of that decision. This group will be good for you.

Accepting love is what you need ask for. It is at the root of all for you. Accepting love is the key to open the door that would lead you back home. You saw yourself in Natalie's book [Awaken from the Dream] yesterday. Indeed you perceive the dream. You understand so many of the dynamics. You are like the one who took part in the deception in protecting the Kingdom, saw the folly, went back to the light, and could not be free because you could not accept love. It is not lack of understanding that keeps you here. It is how deep is your guilt and how great your arrogance in believing you to be a better judge of your worthiness than the Light.

You are a part of our "cluster of light," as it were. Thank you for writing that. We know you did not want to, but it is important that you accept this. The regression Lea facilitated so many years ago gave you the "visual" of the time when we separated. We were never supposed to come with you. You were not to go either. Your guilt and grief are so deep at your perceived entry into this world. We are trying to help you to remember.

You need to shine there, to know your light here. And yet you walk with a darkened cloak, clutched tightly, thinking you can hide your guilt. Feeling that your light gives you away. Your very presence revealing the inappropriateness of your decision to be here. You are like a fish out of water. Ashamed to be recognized. It is time to shed the cloak. You are fooling no one. Only yourself. Those who would recognize your light coming out from under the cloak need your acceptance of Self to be reflected back to them. You are a fish out of water apparent only to other fish! Who would see this and condemn you for their plight as well?

We are all one. Yes. But Ray is not part of this particular light-body. We are all as layers back to the Kingdom, for we are not "there" as well. We travel in groups, much as you do. We overlap groups, as you do. The energy of our group is predominantly "feminine" (to express in a way you can understand) which is why you have chosen to incarnate as a woman most of the time.

We speak to you in simple terms because we know you understand time is neither linear nor real. That is what we meant when we said "Time is not," and this you are grasping. As you reread these words, we know you will understand when we have taken liberty to communicate in the context of the dimension you are in. It is simpler and quicker this way.

Your concern for Sandra and her concern for physical manifestation need not be. You fear that she will be invested or trapped in form, if she can be aware of her creations. But worry not. She is like a child with a new toy, thinking that this will make her happy while she is here, but she will see the distraction and that it does not matter.

Having cannot matter any more than having not. This you know. Those who would "have not" must see that in your plane "having" is the same, though it appears at first to be opposite. It is all right to experience this for it takes this experience to bring the lesson home. When one comes from a place of perceived lack, oft times only "having" what is perceived as lacking can make the point. It could be spiritually arrogant to continue to "do without," to learn this lesson. Part of your martyr or victim role. Ego's trap to keep you here longer. Struggle. Much quicker to "have" and see that it does not hold the meaning for you because it does not hold the Peace.

Remind Sandra of the distinction between "make" and

"create." You give it the word "manifesting," which would seem to guarantee spiritual understanding in this activity, but remember it is merely a fancy word for "make" as long as you are in the dream. This is okay. But do not get caught in the trap of believing these to be your "creations." You are making them. Like mounds of clay. They can only be of the earth and are no measure of your progress, spiritually. Only of your ability to manipulate within the dream. They would merely be part of your lucid dream, for this is your lucid dream. Not so much the dreaming within the dream.

Sandra, Bernadette fears you will get lost with this, as she fears she may get lost with this. She wishes to monitor you as form to herself, as you will both be experiencing instantaneous manifestations. This is a time for both of you to see that "having" is no different than "having not." As long as you are in the dream you do not "have."

A REAL DATE • JOURNAL • Sunday Morning, July 16

What a night! Ray couldn't get out of the dealership on time so we wound up catching the late movie. While I waited for him to pick me up, I ping-ponged from feeling good about the evening to wondering why the hell I ever took action on Lea's suggestion. A good exercise in vulnerability, she said!

Sitting with my hands politely folded in my lap, while the lights dimmed and the movie started, was excruciating. I felt like *throwing up*. I wanted to run out of the theater. All this dialog raced through my head:

"This is crazy! I can't do this. Eighteen years of holding hands in movies. What was I thinking? How did I think I could get through this with my hands in my lap? This hurts too much. Should I reach for his? Hell no! Screw that. I asked him to the movie. I've done my part. It's *his* turn to risk. This vulnerability stuff sucks. I don't need the practice. *He* needs the practice! Lea and Sandra are nuts, and so am I for listening to them!"

Somewhere in all that head talk, Ray took my hand in his. Everything calmed down and I found the peace to go on with our date. After the movie, we browsed through a book store, then went to a coffee house. We talked and drank coffee until they closed. Neither one of us really wanted the evening to end, so we drove around and wound up at the pancake house where we sat so many months ago when this whole separation business started. We talked some more, rediscovering each other over pancakes and omelets. (My comfort food. Ha!) It was 4:00 a.m. when he dropped me off to a Smitty purring loudly at the front door. Maybe this vulnerability stuff works after all.

IN THE MARGINS

So much to write about, but no time! The interview went well. I start my new job in August. Production coordinator. It's not exactly back in advertising, but I will have to use my advertising experience to coordinate layout, design, pre-press, and printing with product deadlines. Going to be wearing a lot of hats. Don't know flip about the phone card business, but will learn.

Joel wasn't real happy, but I didn't expect him to be. Now he is talking as if he's not going to close the showroom, but that's not what I hear on the street. He's not being honest and I can't risk being jobless. I have to take care of myself. Can't rely on Ray's commission checks making up the difference.

Thank you, God. Maybe, now, I can make ends meet – and with a job that will stimulate my mind. A challenge other than this relationship stuff!

JOURNAL • Saturday Morning, July 23

I felt moved last night to read Ray the channeled piece from June the twenty-fifth. He was open to it. After I finished, I asked for his feedback on why it was important for us (for

Spirit) to plant those clues – and where forgiveness would lead us now. We talked about what was going on between us at that time – the emotional outbursts when guilt surfaced, and how harshly we judged ourselves and each other. He agreed that what happened between us was natural – the result of baggage brought into, and dumped on, the marriage. He got it that we both tried to correct our guilt through attacking each other – and that my trying to forgive myself by correcting my flaws really opposed the true nature of the healing that needed to take place.

I asked him to consider his part in this. What affects his decisions and actions, now? What would be different if he chose forgiveness?

SPIRIT DIALOG • Sunday, 5:20 p.m., July 24

There's a lot to take in after Friday evening, Saturday afternoon, and Sunday morning with Ray – *and* my date with Barry, Sunday afternoon. I need to do some catch-up writing but right now, guys, I would rather hear from you.

Where is Ray coming from? Why so much "Ray" on the weekend of my first official date with another man? Any words of comfort, wisdom, or guidance will be appreciated.

You know that Ray is coming back. Ray knew intuitively of your date with Barry. You are connected. He was staking his claim with you, though he feels he has nothing to back it up as he still looks to the material. To the aspect of responsibility. Do not think this is conscious on his part yet. But, as you know, he has never truly left your side. When the door opens, you will have much to share with each other.

It has been necessary for you to see how much you still attack him with your fear for his well being. You see him separated from friends, trying to fit in, and you fear they will not accept him. This is your pity, and yet another attack. Your fear and pity for him is your fear and pity for yourself. You do not want to experience this for yourself and so you project it onto Ray, thinking your projection will make you safe. And yet what you must see is that no one need experience this. Not you. Not he. You fear his inappropriateness as you would fear your own, and so you project this onto Ray as well. You are sharing much, and this is very good, but you need to look at this mirror so you can see him whole. He does not need your fear. He does not need your pity. Can you not see that this weights him down? You say he robs you of energy, but what of you with him?

You are giving more truly to each other now. Ray is walking on eggshells because he still fears his feelings. The time will come soon, however, when he will openly acknowledge his desire to reconcile, though he will still want to keep his space, as you will yours, for you both have much work to do on yourselves. This way is more efficient as you are forced to look, and are in the mode to look, without distracting the other.

Do not worry about breaking Barry's heart. (Ha!) He will enjoy your company but will not want for an exclusive relationship. He has his own intimacy issues. Baggage you do not need. You fear you will have to make a choice, but can you not see you have already made the choice and what is occurring is the coming to pass? You and Ray decided not to leave each other long ago, but you must become more truly yourselves to have something to share with each other. Your guilt, frozen, caused you to slumber back. You are now awakening, thawing, and will come to life again with each other. It matters not who you would choose to be with, so why not with Ray as easily as without Ray?

Be patient. Learn and grow. Remain open and watch love unfold. The time is near. You see that no one projection can give you peace. You see that only the hand of Christ will bring you clear. You attempted to substitute Ray's hand, but now you know that no ego will ever be enough, and that you and Ray may hold the hand of Christ, together. And so long as you see this, yours will be that holy relationship that you prayed for. Witness the miracle. Amen.

JOURNAL • Wednesday, 7:30 a.m., July 27

Have some time here to catch up on the events of this past weekend. An incredible weekend that I do not want to forget.

Friday morning, Ray called. He wanted to drop by after work, to give me some money for bills. I agreed. Natalie and I were on the phone when he called to let me know he was on his way. Said he was running late and hadn't eaten – had I? He was conversationally "wondering" about where *we* could eat. I had Natalie on hold, so I told him to come over and *we* would decide when he arrived.

It was cute! He brought coupons for my favorite soup and salad place. Went to the one by the mall. His treat. While we were eating, he said he wanted to show me his apartment – but didn't want me to get "the wrong idea." I laughed at the thought of what the wrong idea might be. So many to choose! He also wanted to go by the dealership to say his final good-byes to some of the guys he'd missed earlier. (I can't believe we're both changing jobs. Didn't know he was looking.) When we got there he introduced me as his wife. I am not sure what, if anything, that means. He should have dropped that part, based on my "do not consider me your wife any longer" anniversary speech. Had he not really *heard* what I'd said, or figured that it was different now? Or did he just introduce me that way out of habit?

Went back to his apartment. Chatted about all kinds of stuff – the stray cat he's feeding, his roommate, Josh's acting class. That's when I read the channeled piece to him. Spirit had given the nudge earlier so I had stuffed a copy in my purse. Left it with him. Also shared some of the information I'd received the following Sunday morning regarding Shelly and the frozen guilt. Don't know how much he really grasped, but he didn't balk at any of it. We called it a night and he took me home. Figured that was all I'd hear from him for the rest of the weekend. Wrong!

About 1:30, Saturday afternoon, Ray called again. He

wanted to take me over to see his friend's artwork and studio set up. He thought it would be a good field trip for our creativity. We picked up pizza – my treat this time – and went on to Lou's. It was a very inspirational visit. Lou seems to live his art – like breathing. No big deal. No performance anxiety. He just does it, and if he doesn't like it, he does it over.

On the way back home – my home – Ray and I talked about what went into his decision to quit the dealership. I knew he hated it there, and all the questionable business practices, but the more I heard about the new job, the more uncomfortable I got. Could not put my finger on why exactly. I just felt myself getting anxious, concerned about his making the right choice for the right reason. Did not want to pass my anxiousness on to him so I chose *only* to share about using forgiveness as a tool in decision making. About how decisions based on guilt, anger, or fear bring more of the same, while forgiveness allows for releasing destructive patterns. Said that I knew he would do what was right for him and left it at that.

When he expressed a desire that we go down to explore the Highlands that evening, I became painfully aware of our pattern for killing time – and how good we were at distracting each other when there were important things that required our attention – and said so. He acknowledged the pattern, agreed that particular night was not the best time, and we said good-bye. All I could think about was how I needed to get out of that car before I got into trouble. My anxiety was increasing with the compulsion to *help* him with this job decision, and I needed some serious quiet time to look at why. He pulled out of the driveway with no clue about how disturbed or perplexed I was. Thank God!

Sunday morning, while I was getting ready to leave for The Course group, I saw where my fear *for* Ray was really an attack *on* Ray. How *always* my fears for him, his decisions, what others thought of him were attacks. When I hold onto these fears I don't trust him – or God. And when I don't trust – when I'm feeling insecure about something – it does not matter whether I'm protecting, defending, or attacking. It's all the same. Relief from the intense anxiety that lingered came shortly after this awareness.

Walked in late and was surprised to see Ray sitting at the table. Saturday afternoon he had said he might try the group some Sunday, but I guess I didn't think he'd really show up. Cliff and Natalie were there. Natalie knew about Friday night, but I had not had a chance to tell her about Saturday afternoon. Sandra and Adam were there also. It was a curiously entertaining hour, as the four of them knew about my blind date with Barry later that afternoon.

Ray's appearance brought an amusing twist to my plans. Afterward, we went out for our usual breakfast at the log cabin – with Ray joining us, of course. I felt a little nervous because I'd scheduled my lunch date with Barry for 1:30 – something I had *not* shared with Ray in our time together over the weekend. I felt very split with so much "Ray" on the same weekend I had given myself permission to officially date another man.

If that weren't agitation enough, I started obsessing on how Ray would fit back in – not just with the gang at the table – but with everybody.

Ray ordered a big breakfast and was insistent that we also split an order of pancakes. I'd planned on eating very light but he kept feeding me from his plate. Try this. Try that. This is good. Just have a bite. So much for lunch with Barry! It was as if he knew my plans and was trying to sabotage them. I could tell that Sandra and Adam were rolling at the hilarity of it all, and I didn't dare look directly at them. Sandra later pointed out that feeding me was an intimate act, not something a man who saw himself as truly separated and heading for divorce would do. We talked about how my fear regarding Ray's not "fitting in" later turned into feeling sorry for him, and noted how that *too* was an attack.

I am both amazed and overwhelmed at ego's subtle persistence in attacking Ray under the guise of concern and love. A real eye-opener for me, an awareness I need to keep.

The date with Barry was pleasant but anti-climatic after the morning I'd had. Sipped my wine, picked at my salad, and worked very hard to stay in the moment. Occasionally the jukebox played a song that made me think of Ray. But the real killer was when I heard Sade singing, "There must have been an angel by my side."[*] When she got to that part about "built a bridge to your heart all the way" I wanted to laugh *and* cry. The work of our angels! I think they did it just to amuse themselves while I squirmed. Felt my eyes get watery. Don't know if Barry noticed. If he did, he didn't let on. I really had to focus hard on the conversation. We talked about going out again. I guess I'll give him another shot, to be fair. We didn't meet on the best of days. Don't think we share enough interests though. Maybe he's just too normal.

Ray called early Monday morning. He'd decided to give this new company a shot and was comfortable with it. The idea came up again about forgiveness being the basis for decision making. It clicked. I felt his "ah-ha." We talked about how so many of our decisions were based on guilt, and how that might have played into why we never achieved the success we thought we would. I told him about my forgiveness meditations that always seemed to exclude our first two years of marriage in New York and how I'd wondered why. He reflected that perhaps those were years of grace.

I wondered out loud: if we were to choose forgiveness, could we go back to those first two years and progress from that point of grace? Would we find our passion for each other? Our spontaneity? Our love?

He was quiet, and in the silence I immediately filled with fear. I'd revealed too much and felt totally vulnerable at his lack of response. I couldn't stand it, so I tried to fill the gap. Tried covering up the fear with chit chat about how

---

[*]Sade, Love Deluxe, *Kiss of Life* (Sony Music Entertainment, UK Limited, 1992)

good it was to have our own space – to be starting new jobs – anything that would make me appear to be unattached. I was angry with myself for being so revealing and was even more angry for filling the gap, for not waiting to see how he *would* respond. After we hung-up I went into major ego attack. Called him right back. Twice. But there was no answer. I was frantic.

It was getting close to my tanning appointment. I considered canceling, but this was to be a special treat to myself. I decided getting out might do me good and help me switch gears, but that's where I had my black hole experience. Lying in the bed felt strangely like lying in a coffin. The tanning lights disappeared. Everything got dark. I was slipping into another dimension. Panic and fear were all I felt. Terror that I was being pulled into my own personal black hole somewhere out there in the universe, a place where no one, not even God, could find me. Lost for all eternity. Conscious darkness and isolation for all eternity! In my mind, I cried out for help. I prayed. I pleaded. The light started filtering back in. I knew I'd had a powerful experience but was too shaken to entertain what it meant. I trembled all the way home and couldn't get rid of the deep sense of isolation I felt. I went through a mental list of all those dear to me, reaching for them the way one who is drowning would reach for a lifeline, but could make no connections in my heart. The black hole was somehow linked to my conversation with Ray. To my filling the gap when he fell silent on the phone.

When I got home, I called him again. This time he answered. All I could say was, "I don't know why I'm calling you. I feel vulnerable for what I asked you and I'm paying dearly for it with a major ego attack." I cried. Told him about being sucked into the darkness, and jabbered on about how isolated I felt from everyone and everything – until he stopped me. He wouldn't let me fixate on feeling abandoned by anyone. He was very strong and certain in his response.

He drew it all back to us and said, "What happened, happened between you and me, and I'm not threatened by it. I feel blessed for the time we've spent together this weekend. For our conversation this morning."

Then he admitted that he had cried in the silence. The gap that I had tried to cover up. What a shock! That he would have cried never occurred to me. I didn't ask him why. It was enough to know that he had, and the knowing calmed me down. I thanked him. He thanked me. We hung up and I went out to have lunch with his Mom. That evening, he called to make sure I was still okay.

I know, as I'm writing all this, I'm still looking for signs that he is coming back. I've been told, and yet I keep wondering. Is it now? Is it now? I'm tired of this. I'm tired of being alone. I'm tired of sharing these awarenesses from a distance. I don't know where his heart is. If I knew his heart was with mine, I could relax. I could have peace.

There I go. Flipping it around. Placing my peace outside – again. It is not where his heart is, but mine that should concern me. Ray is not the cause of my peace. Spirit, I know he is not. But I still buy into believing that he is when I miss him. That's just where I am.

JOURNAL • Thursday Afternoon, July 28

Some points I need to think about, that came up in session with Sandra.

- I need to look at why and where I fill gaps of silence with action. Who am I protecting when I do it? Ray or myself? How does filling the gap maintain the "specialness" the Course refers to? What would happen if I didn't fill the gap?
- What does my concern about other's views of Ray reflect of my own fear about Ray, were he to come back? Where am I projecting onto friends and family *my* fears regarding his ability and willingness to carry his weight in the marriage?

JOURNAL • Thursday Evening, July 28

Ray just dropped off an acting book. He felt it would help me in Josh's class. I told him it could wait until I got back from Florida. Maybe he just wanted to do something for me. Or, maybe he wanted to see me before I fly out tomorrow morning. I know he's excited about my taking Josh's class. I also think it surprised him. I almost sensed he was living vicariously through me – and grieving his decision to step away from acting when all this separation stuff started in February.

Leaving tomorrow to see the folks without him feels so weird. Another first, and an awkward one at that. With all that's happened, there's been no contact between Ray and any member of my family since March when Peggy left. There have been so many mixed feelings with family and friends: about this separation, the other woman, our opening the lines of communication again. No one has said a word to me, but I get a definite sense of who is *for* and who is *against* our getting back together. I'm grateful they've kept their thoughts to themselves.

This change of scenery will be good before I start my new job. I'm feeling pretty strong. Certainly stronger than I was when Mom came up. Amazing how much growth in so little time. It will be good for the folks to see me this way, Dad especially. I think he still sees me as the victim – and, with all the work I've done, I don't believe I'm reflecting *that* anymore.

> *Open your heart. This is about your heart.
> About forgiveness that frees you to love truly.*

You can see that you must wholly forgive. Any part that you would choose to hold back will manifest as yet another experience to work through and we know you tire of that.

AUGUST

A NOD FROM HEAVEN • JOURNAL • Monday Afternoon, August 1

Home sweet home. Could not have written that five months ago! It's a good feeling.

Want to get a couple of thoughts down from the trip while they're still fresh in my mind. Fully intended to write while I was there but it was so great seeing everybody – and being away – that it just didn't happen.

All the years that Ray and I drove because the folks were too close to justify the expense of plane fare! Flying is definitely the way to go, at least for a long weekend trip like this. It was nice not arriving road weary. Mom picked me up from the airport. God, it was good to see her standing there when I got off the plane. I am struggling to find the words here. I mean, there was nothing new revealed – she's up on everything – but something happened when our eyes met. Two women – silently, powerfully – witnessing, celebrating, sharing – strength, courage, growth. It was an awesome feeling. And I am grateful to know it.

Got a big hug from Dad when we arrived at the house. He looked a little surprised and relieved, though he covered it well. It was cute. As I carried my bags to the bedroom, I could hear him say to Mom in this hushed voice, "She looks good." Almost like, "Damn. How'd she do that?"

Here comes Smitty, trying to curl up on my journal. Guess he missed me, though I'm sure Aunts Natalie and Angie did a fair job of spoiling him. Cute, now he's rolled over onto his back beside me, covering his face with his paws. What a pleasure he is!

Anyway, back to my thoughts. Flying into Orlando, I was looking out the window and noticed the sun was at an angle that allowed me to see the plane's shadow cast on the landscape below. I was mesmerized watching the shadow play over the fields and houses as we cruised by. At some point, I stopped thinking of it as a shadow and viewed it as *the plane*. As we approached the landing strip, the shadow plane got larger and larger and soon we merged. Then Spirit interjected the thought, "And that is how it happens." I knew they were talking about how this "dream" became real to us. We were mesmerized with our shadows on the landscape as they danced and played and shifted forms. At some point, we forgot who was doing the looking and where we were looking from and saw *only* the shadows. We merged without conscious awareness and got lost in form, where shadow and content *seemed* to become one.

Funny how long it took to get out that thought. The actual revelation was a split second "Ah-ha." Like an electric shock.

Another interesting revelation came on my flight back, again as I looked out the window. I was mesmerized this time by the fantastic cloud formations. Landscapes passing by me, just as intriguing as the shadow plane. Magical castles and bridges, hills and valleys, gaps of blue that looked like lakes surrounded by snow capped mountains. Then I saw it. A rainbow. A big, bright, beautiful "hello" spanning across one of those gaps of blue tucked boldly and neatly between the clouds. And I realized, I would never have seen that rainbow from the ground because there were clouds beneath it. At that point, it dawned on me that I had been looking for a rainbow all spring and summer. Not consciously, but instinctively. Countless times looking up to the sky, hoping to see one. A nod from heaven that everything would be all right. I knew this was my rainbow. That it had been waiting all summer for me to raise my vision. That I was being told to rise above my clouds and try a new vantage point, because a whole different perspective was necessary to see.

Great sign. Thanks, guys. I got it.

IN THE MARGINS

Red flag. My new job is bringing up some uncomfortable challenges, and I'm a little nervous about what I am really walking into. Cheryl, my boss-to-be called tonight and wanted to know if I could start tomorrow. She sounded a bit stressed. My first thought was to say "Yes" because I didn't have any specific plans for the day. I took a deep breath – silently, of course – and told her that wouldn't be possible but that I would be there Wednesday as originally agreed.

God, that was tough. Simple truth is that I wanted one more day to myself. Actually, I would have liked a whole week off between jobs but she was so eager to have me start when I hired in, that I compromised.

Damn. Saying no has never been easy for me. Saying no *for* me has never been easy. I can say it if I have an outside commitment – but a commitment to myself doesn't count as valid. I am not going to start this new job off on that foot.

Ray called right after I hung up with Cheryl. He started his job today. Seems they misrepresented the commission structure and stability of the company. Found myself feeling very agitated with him in the conversation. I know he was not asking anything of me but my compulsion to fix came up. Didn't want to sound as snippy as I felt so told him I was tired from the trip and needed to get some rest.

I just don't want to deal with any of this job stuff right now.

SPIRIT DIALOG • Tuesday, August 2

Really feel a need to connect. Please, share with me any information you have about my new job, Ray's new job, Ray, myself, anything that is pertinent.

This is so formal an approach to a connection with us, but we understand that this you need, as you needed to see and touch your mother – and your father needed to see and touch you, to gain in the reassurance that you are indeed all right. But it is happening for you so spontaneously that this manner of sharing continues to limit you. One day you shall know what you think you know and you shall not be bound by such limited perceptions of communication.

You are at yet another crossroads and you see it matters not which direction you take, so long as you think you are in this world. But you must choose a direction, and so you sit. This is good. Today was meant for just that. Sit and simply feel what you feel for you know not what this place is. Yet you recognize its import.

Behold, each day you converse with Ray you see Spirit at work. And yet you seem surprised, though this is what you have yearned for. Funny that you don't know how to feel when these opportunities for honest exchange present themselves. This is why you are in Josh's acting class. You have so many canned feelings, as offensive to you as canned laughter on your television shows. Insincere and contrived. Allow yourself to "be" and feel what comes as a result. You will be far more true to yourself in that than in feigning happiness, or relief, or irritation, or self-restraint, or whatever you might think you should feel.

Forgiveness is living in the moment.

You know there is nothing that you can do for Ray except to see your own reflection in him and love that. He senses this. The words necessary for you to share with him will come to you in the moment. There is no script for this, Bernadette. This you have chosen. There is no script, which is why you cannot project. Results are in the moment absolutely. Be grateful, for in this you will find your freedom. And so shall Ray, as he chooses to acknowledge another perception. This phase will be over within the month. What you share with him, you share with you.

Shall you embark upon this new job in guilt or forgiveness? How easy it is to fall back into the old way. You saw this today at breakfast with Lea. Last night's exasperation with Ray reflected your struggle with the decision to hold to your original agreement with Cheryl. Your desire to "leave Ray with his own mess," as you so dramatically expressed to Lea, originated from the fear that Cheryl's need should override yours. That you did not deserve this day to "be," as you had no specific plans to "do." Your feelings of agitation regarding Ray's job situation exposed your guilt. A guilt that surfaced with Cheryl's request, not Ray's call. The impatience that you projected onto Ray comes from your own lack of vision for yourself. This awareness was skirting just outside your field. Forgiveness requires not a sacrifice.

"Why is he not getting it? How can I help him to get it?" Ha! Replace "he" with "I" and you have basis to grow. Ray benefits from this awareness right now. Mark the time.

It is all about forgiveness. It matters not the form the symbols take, but rather in deciphering their meaning to each, and their perception. Lea has already made her choice and this disturbs you, as you fear you are reflecting yourself and Ray in her situation. And yet, you too have made your choice, and though you choose to be with Ray you also fear this will be so. Can you not see you project this fear onto Lea? You cannot imagine being with Ray anymore than you can imagine Lea with Nathan, as the manner of "being with" is so far outside the realm of your experience or memory of a time when this could be so – in peace – that it defies you in ego. Which is why you must be in the moment, as she must as well. Perfectly in the moment, and in touch with feelings now. Not based on how things used to feel and so "should" feel today. The form the symbol takes is not important. And yet we do recognize your need for that which is familiar. We do work with you where you are. Are you not grateful?

JOURNAL • Friday, August 5

Met Barry tonight for dinner. Gave it another shot. He is very nice but we are just too different. Even if Ray and I weren't conversing, he still would not interest me. Apparently my raging hormones aren't so apt to run me as wild as I thought. I am still pretty picky. That's a relief.

We went to a great little Mexican restaurant, though. Excellent margaritas. Will have to call for a girl's night out and go back. Best part of the evening is right now – at home, listening to my music and dancing in the dark. Now there's some progress. I am my own best date!

JOURNAL • Friday, August 12

This is going to be a different journal entry. For the past couple of days, bits and pieces of verse have been popping in. Like words to a song or a poem. I finally started jotting them down just to see where they would go. Was surprised with what came up. I have never thought of myself as a poet, but this experience felt like a poet's process – not like it was channeled – more like a collaboration. Like the words themselves had a life of their own and wished to be spoken. It's been healing, satisfying in an unfamiliar sort of way.

Really don't know how to properly structure it as prose or poetry, so will make up my own rules, I guess. Listen to me. Making excuses like I'm back in school.

Here it is, copied from a kajillion scribbled notes.

THE WHISPER

The trail of the fool,
following tears and laughter of days gone by
or yet to be?
Paths traveled once, twice, countless times,
each ending always at the same place.
The true path starting, not at the crossroads
but at the heart,

where all that is remains ever present,
awaiting but a seeming return.

I look for you without, and yet carry you within.
I run from you in troubled dreams,
and yet seek your comfort
here,
there perhaps,
and still another place,
when all the while you are as near as the beat of my heart.

Alone.
Nights come. Nights come to pass.
The moon, the stars, seem closer to me than you.
Where is your heart?
Where is mine,
that we cannot seem to find comfort
in our company shared?

This fool. This journey.
Path chosen.
Dream upon dream.
Seeking the source of a reflection that beckons
your Spirit mirror to my own.
Dare we look beyond shattered, fear-filled years?

My heart yearns for the You
whom I have not yet clearly seen in this dream.
Vague rememberings
whisper
from a part of me that will not be still.

"Awaken, dear one.
The journey of the fool is over,
for it never truly began."

EYES WIDE OPEN • JOURNAL • Saturday, August 13

I have really fallen off my writing. Between learning a new job and Ray steadily moving back into my days with phone calls, and my nights with dates, there is hardly time to stop and record my feelings about anything. It seems all I can do is live my life as it happens. I guess I'm following Spirit's advice to be present in the present.

I'm in awe of it all. Everything feels so new. So fragile. And yet, with that newness comes a strength. Like a bone that's grown back stronger at the break. I was broken, and now that I am out of the cast I'm feeling everything. Every movement, temperature change, breeze, itch – right up to my hair standing on end. I'm keenly aware of each little shift. Every old taken-for-granted sensation is new and fresh.

Each time Ray calls is like the first time. Each date, like a first date. Only more poignant somehow, because it's with eyes wide open. No smoke screens. No illusions. We have a history that won't let us play that, and yet how many couples get to have that first date twice? Court each other twice? Consciously challenged by what there is yet to forgive but choosing to release the past to a present, tender, scary-as-hell moment. No distracting sexual games or expectations. Just holding hands and being in the other's presence. Allowing Spirit to connect us.

Fear rushes in. Do we have what we need to make it work this time or are we just kidding ourselves? What if he's all for it, and I decide I'm not? What if we get back together and fall into our old ruts? What if, after all that has happened for me to find myself, I lose myself again and don't notice?

We could just forgive, forget, and go our separate ways. Wouldn't a fresh start with someone else be easier in the long run?

JOURNAL • Monday Evening, August 15

Last night's conversation with Ray marked a monumental point in our communication. On the phone for four hours! The issues we found ourselves talking about just seemed to slip in. I was so absolutely honest and on target with what I said that it kind of threw me. I knew what to say, when to say it, and how. Spirit was definitely with us. And Ray's Higher Self was very present. Any number of times he could have hung up on me, but he stayed right in there. Present. Not defensive. All the excuses, the rationalizations, the "yes buts" called out, recognized for what they were, and stripped of their power.

At one point, I silently drew a Rune to make sure we were doing the right thing and not just playing an ego game. I got *Breakthrough. Transformation day.*[*] It acknowledged one moment, if recognized and acted upon, that changes the course of life forever. The kind of moment that calls for radical trust – and absolute faith. With that, I continued on.

We called up a lot. All the read-between-the-lines stuff that we had never openly owned. Years worth. The work I'd been doing with Sandra – all my writing – came into play. I knew, he knew, we could go no farther without giving voice to all of what stood between us and our ability to be in a loving relationship.

I had to ask him if he'd ever really – honestly – asked himself why he lost his feelings for me? Why he was afraid to let passion and spirit merge in one relationship?

I know we must have hit on something because I called him at work today and he wasn't there. He was home, sick as a dog. But you know what? I feel great! Like The Course says, "Nothing real can be threatened."

---

[*] Rune drawing paraphrased from Ralph Blum, *The Book of Runes* (New York, 1987, Oracle Books / St. Martin's Press)

THE HOLY INSTANT • JOURNAL
Monday, August 22

Another weekend spent together. Started Saturday night at his place. We shopped for groceries, made supper, and had a picnic on his bedroom floor. He was so proud of the space he'd created for himself. His personal environment. It showed me how much we had both gotten lost in the marriage. Kinda made me wonder if neither of us felt "at home" all those years, who was living there? Watching him move about the apartment and play with Abigail, the stray cat he'd unofficially adopted (because his roommate doesn't like cats), gave me a different sense of compassion for him. I was really seeing him.

Before I went home that evening, we talked about taking a drive up to the mountains the next day. But Sunday morning it was raining so hard, we canceled. He came over to the house around noon, and we were in the process of trying to decide what to do when I felt the urge to read him a section out of The Course. While I was reading, the room seemed to get brighter, as if the sun had come out from behind the clouds. But it was still pouring rain. When I finished, I looked up. Ray was staring at me. His eyes were bright. I felt their intensity. I just looked at him – afraid to speak, afraid to break the moment. He was seeing. And I knew he was seeing me, or us, in a way that he may never have before. When he finally spoke, he confirmed it and added that he believed he had just experienced a holy instant.

Shortly after, the rain stopped, the sun came out, and we went down to the Highlands for food and fun. We'd won twenty-seven dollars on a scratch-off ticket, so dinner was on the state lottery. Actually, it felt more like a gift from heaven. An approving nod from Spirit to go out and enjoy each other as we finished out the weekend. We'd done our work.

Forgiveness is living in the moment.

Forgiveness requires not a sacrifice.

SEPTEMBER

THE SILVER LINING • JOURNAL • Thursday Evening, September 1

    Definitely like my new job, in spite of the hurdle created by Lenny's quitting a week after I started. Kinda wonder if I was set up, though. Like, they suspected he was going to quit and that's why they hired me. Really put me under pressure to learn as much as I could from him, before his last day. I'm not so worried about the layout and design end of it, or the pre-press. That stuff I know. It's all the particulars that I'm nervous about. Who are the clients? What are their personalities? Their needs? Who are the suppliers? Is their service consistent? What jobs are in progress? In what stage? I was really hoping to get a sense of what was in existence before I started implementing changes or setting up procedures. But there doesn't seem to be a system – at least not one that will support the kind of volume we're heading into. Everything is way too scattered.

    Last Thursday, I made the decision not to wait for them to hire a replacement for Lenny before restructuring. I gave myself permission to trust my ability to organize, to start from scratch and allow my system to evolve as my understanding of their business grew. Am I ever glad I did, because it gave me the emotional buffer I needed when they informed me today that they wanted to see how I could do on my own.

    So, the art department with its one apprentice has now merged with my production department – which really isn't in full operation yet. I don't know enough about what has been going on here to intelligently argue the logic, but the good news is I get a raise to compensate for the additional responsibilities. As soon as I figure out what they are, I'll know if it's a fair one.

This job is starting to mimic my life. Let go of existing structures (the past) and rebuild based on current understanding (be in the present) while upside down (that's the trust God part). Aside from these initial challenges and the fact that in my scramble to deal with them I haven't had time to write or meditate, this job is just what I prayed for. I am using my creativity in problem solving with people who openly appreciate my talent and respect my input. The casual family atmosphere is an added bonus.

Ray threw a bit of a curve into my work situation today as well. With his office so close, he wanted to pick me up for lunch and come in to meet the gang. Told him I couldn't. That I was working through because of the holiday weekend coming up. How do I tell him they don't know he exists? And what do I tell them? When I hired in, they didn't ask, I didn't offer. I wanted my privacy. But, now, I am really feeling awkward. Like I'm keeping secrets every time Ray and I meet for lunch. Don't have a problem with telling them now. It's just how, what, and when to say it. "Hey, guys, by the way, I'm sorta married – and this fellow is my kinda husband." Ha!

Guess I will decide my approach after I see how we do this weekend, and the odds of having a good weekend will, no doubt, be improved if I purge some of my feelings, on paper, about this stuff going on with Ray. I'm working very hard not to blurt out my concerns about his new job. Have met his boss and do not get a good hit. He's likable enough but there is something that doesn't feel right. Already, they're changing the commission structure agreement, and one of Ray's commission checks has bounced. He's giving them a little more time because this is a new operation. Says they are just working out the bugs. I hope he's right.

Maybe what's really bothering me about all this is that Ray's old agent called out of the blue to see if Ray wanted to audition for a film. If he didn't get a part, he would have the option of doing some extensive background or stand-in work. It's a big production and they need tons of people. The catch is, it's a long project. Even if he only acted as an extra, it would mean extending full time availability for a couple of months. Ray would have to give up this new job. So, he turned it down. Said it felt too much like the old days. Like chasing rainbows. That acting was too unreliable as a professional pursuit. He wants to experience some financial stability. To be able to plan, and budget, and get out of the hole. I know where he's coming from and really do honor his intentions. His heart is in the right place, concerning his sense of fiscal responsibility, but I can't let go of the feeling that this is a sign. That acting is not a dream he is supposed to set aside. It's weird that I'm the one grieving this decision while he seems to have peace with it.

Help me to trust his process. If he is not to give up acting, another opportunity will present itself and/or this current job situation will fizzle. I have to let go of the feeling that his decision represents a sacrifice.

SPIRIT DIALOG • Friday, September 2

Spirit, I feel so strange tonight. What an odd mix of emotions! Tomorrow, Ray and I head up to the mountains for the weekend. Our first sleep-over since we separated. Suddenly this feels like a big jump from hugs and kisses – and holding hands. It seemed like a good idea when we planned it, but now I feel sick. I can't stop crying. My whole body is buzzing. What's going on?

We have never left your side. There has been much to do.
This weekend will be good. The buzzing you feel is nervous energy. Ray does not mean to you what he did before and that frightens you, as you cannot imagine a way of relating so different from what you always accepted. Allow. Allow. That is all you need do. Simply allow peace to flow into your perceived union.
Your ego grieves and is afraid. Be aware of its ways. It will sabotage. Ray's bounced check. Ray's agent. Leave them be! He

will invite you in. Your ego wants him to. Do not accept the invitation to worry. Allow love to reflect and you will be just fine. Go in peace. This is your blessed moment.

JOURNAL • Tuesday Morning, September 6

What a wonderful weekend! I know Ray wanted me to spend the night Friday, but I am glad I kept that time and space for myself. I felt much better for it Saturday morning. Our drive up was great. Very relaxed. It was so good to be in the mountains again. They really settle me. Don't know why.

Was a bit scary when we got to Cherokee and couldn't find a room. Didn't think about it being Labor Day weekend. We finally located a little motel with just one vacancy outside town. Possibly the last one in the whole area. Shelter secured, we went out to explore and enjoy a full day of taking in the sights, the fresh mountain air, and the newness of each other.

Then came Saturday night and the motel room. We'd taken each moment that day as it presented itself – and this definitely ranked as the most awkward. We agreed we would share the bed – but the heat was off regarding sex. Neither one of us was in a place to consummate (or would that be re-consummate) our relationship. Taking it slow felt best. There were too many feelings that we still needed to address. Plus, there was the awkwardness of my wanting to practice safe sex. A condom between us definitely would have invited an entourage of emotions that we didn't need to work through on that night. I told him I had gotten tested for HIV after he'd moved out and had been cleared. He had yet to be tested. Ironic when I think of how we wound up in the sack on our first date. Who would have thought that, technically married, we'd find ourselves delaying sex. A caution that would have been more appropriate then. Guess we got a second chance to see what it would feel like to make a healthier decision.

Funny, how we think of sex as being the ultimate expression of intimacy, and yet, Saturday night, the level of intimacy our *honesty* allowed far surpassed any sexual fantasies I might have held for the evening. It was a night of precious baby steps. Both of us careful not to offer more than we felt ready to handle. Should we light the candles and incense we each secretly tucked into our bags and set the mood with ambient music? Or kick up the florescents and set out the chess game? Should I wear nightgown *A*, that tastefully revealed a re-emerging slender body? Or *B*, that casually hinted at it without the see-through quality? Gut checks allowed for candles, incense, music, and nightgown *B*. (*A* was too much of a stretch for *me* to handle.)

But the sweetest of all the vulnerabilities expressed that night was when Ray risked to pull out the massage oil he'd bought for me last January, just before the shit hit the fan. The oil that was in the little brown bag I had made such a horrible fuss over. There are no words that I could possibly write here that would come anywhere close to expressing my absolute amazement, my awe, at the perfectly miraculous significance of his choice to bring that bottle. That he even kept it – unopened – was evidence of grace. Of a power at work in our lives in spite of us. A massage with that oil was long overdue. Forgiveness was at hand. (Pun intended!) We took turns – giving – receiving – and fell asleep in each other's arms.

We spent Sunday morning by the river that ran through town – meditating, sketching, taking it all in. Left Cherokee early afternoon and stopped in Dillsboro for dinner. Got home late. Ray spent Sunday night with me. (Boy, was Smitty pleased!) Monday morning he insisted we join forces in reclaiming my overgrown backyard. Who was I to argue?

As he was packing up to leave that night, he sat me on the bed and took my hand in his. He had the wedding band (that I'd thrown into March's box of goodies) poised at the tip of my ring finger. I was shocked. The moment I'd been praying for! He asked if I would allow him to place the ring on my finger and accept it as a sign of his recommitment. I hesitated, not because I doubted him or myself, but because I wanted to be absolutely conscious of what it meant to say "Yes." Just as he was absolutely conscious of what it meant to ask.

We agreed it was time for us to start seeing Sandra and address our issues – as a couple. (Especially if we ever wanted to have sex again. Ha!) And we talked about when he might move back in. I want to take this slowly. Get a few sessions tucked under our belt. Then decide when the right time is.

Guess I better tell the gang at work about Ray. They might wonder about the ring – if they notice. Maybe I will tell them I eloped with a guy I met in the mountains.

BEYOND THE FEAR • SPIRIT DIALOG
Thursday, September 22

Cannot believe it's almost the end of the month. Started rereading the earlier writings from Spirit and find that I miss sharing our connection in that manner. I know I'm still plugged in, but that paper trail holds a special feeling for me.

So much has happened in so little time. None of it recorded. How do I go back and retrace the events? And, if my power is in the present, as Spirit has said, does it really matter?

I still have concerns about our financial situation and the stress that comes with it. So many things to point a finger at! My raise was not enough. Ray's boss is still bouncing checks. The dealership misrepresented the program car Ray bought when he was working for them. It has a bent frame and is not safe. He can't get out of his lease at the apartment – blah, blah, blah!

Fear and guilt trying to manifest that all too familiar attack and punishment cycle! Can we really dig ourselves out of this hole? Ego chatters on with all kinds of things. "This is going to be too much work. The two of you are not cut out for this. Besides, he doesn't really love you. He does not love anyone. Why don't you wait for someone who *can* love?"

When the thoughts come in, I try to simply observe and let them float past.

You and Raymond have tried many times for this place you are in now. This crossroads is not new to either of you. You have been here with each other, as well as perceived others. Heaven rejoices. You have chosen for Love, though you know it not in the place you are in. We rejoice with you, and more so than you, for you still suffer under the dictates of ego meandering.

The hesitation you feel is natural for one so young, but you grow rapidly. Do not fear Ray's moving in "too soon." You are progressing so quickly that only in your time reference does this action appear quick. And yet, to your growth in spirit, it is in slow motion. When your energies are brought together, hold on tight and have faith for the final major clearance shall commence.

Do not fear, but rather continue to love. Listen to your inner voices. The guidance is there beyond the fear. Look to Love, and rest in peace.

Love and Light. The Gifted Ones.

> *Do not fear, but rather continue to love. Listen to your inner voice. The guidance is there beyond the fear. Look to Love.*

OCTOBER

BELOVED • JOURNAL • Saturday Morning, October 1

What an absolutely gorgeous morning! The eastern light is dancing through the branches of the tree just outside the window casting lacy shadows as it cuts a path across the living room wall. The front door is wide open and every once in a while a wisp of a breeze makes its way through the screen, carrying the scent of autumn leaves warming to the sun. I was going to use this little bit of time to catch up on some writing, but I've just been sitting here taking it all in. Everything feels so crisp, so exquisite. It's as if the morning is on parade.

Shortly, Ray will be pulling up the driveway and we will start the process of moving him back in. Amazing grace! I think I'll just be still and bask in the miracle.

JOURNAL • Saturday Evening

All moved in, but not unpacked. The day was too pretty to stay inside. Ray's boxes are stacked everywhere among my things. It will be curious to see how we choose to put our pieces together this time. Where the give and take will be, in creating this new space from the inside out. I know there are those who might question our judgment in this reconciliation, in his moving back so soon; but, right now, I don't care. My honey has found his way home, and I am grateful.

SPIRIT DIALOG • Wednesday, October 26

October the twenty-sixth? Have I gotten that busy?

Such a strange evening. Ray shared with me that Shelly paged him today.

What an interesting range of feelings *that* brought on! My first reaction was one of casual confidence topped with an "Oh really, why would she be calling you?" No suspicion or fear behind it at all. That was an excellent feeling.

He said she wanted to know if he was still selling cars. She had a friend who was in the market for one. He told her no – and that we were back together. I felt like his decision to share her phone call with me, and my peace with it, allowed a deepening in our commitment to let go of our fears and guilt and choose love in rediscovering each other.

Of course, ego couldn't leave it at that. An hour later my stomach started doing flips. I was on the roller coaster. I wanted to scream. I wanted to cry. What an intriguing contrast to the calm of the previous hour! To be in touch with those feelings and not try to control or suppress them – or attack Ray with them. No need to blame. No need to fix. I chose to simply have, observe, and *be* with them. I knew they were part of a dying core belief that no longer served me. And to be able to share that openly with Ray, without going through the attack-defense cycle, was amazing as well.

Funny, my old boss called this morning to see how I was doing. I told him that Ray and I were back together, and he said, "So, you've won." I never once thought in terms of "over her," though I know that is what he meant. It's been about winning over me and all the years of fear and guilt that colored my choices. Even with tonight's mini ego attack, the fact that I could be calm and casual (confident in the relationship) first and find myself on the roller coaster as an *afterthought*, tells me I have won in a way that really counts.

Celebrate. Celebrate, dear one! It matters not what you think you see "out there," but what you know you feel inside. There is a commitment that has occurred on behalf of yourself and your brother. The peace you feel, when you feel it, is real and is not denial. Look about you and know the love in what you reflect, at this very moment, as pleasing.

Raymond will not betray you. He never did. Even Shelly's call now acts as confirmation, not conflagration. This, that you know together, is far greater than you have known to this point, in this dream. There is no turning back, and this Shelly must see in line with her own ability to interpret. She has done you a good turn. Your union does her so as well. This she needs to know.

You see as you must and are not so heavily invested in fear as you were. This is good. What you see are your own walls opposing peace. Remember that they are your walls and you will see them taken down. Some will dissolve quickly. Some will be one painful brick at a time.

Call the vet on behalf of Ray's stray cat, Abigail. You will know what to do as you go. You have already made a connection with her. Why pretend you have not? The worst that can happen is that you are out a little money, and that you are already. Perhaps Smitty would like a friend. At the very least, she will be cleaned up and ready for her new home. It is time for something different, Bernadette. This action on Abigail's behalf is merely another avenue by which you show your willingness to trust. It is not the outcome but the act. Do the footwork. Let us take care of the rest.

You and Raymond need only go with the flow at work. The mirror is the same for both. You have covered all bases. Only in your combined puzzle pieces will you see the truth. This must be so. There are no coincidences. Take heart in that. Look at your respective situations and forgive. The next move will be apparent and natural.

Take heart! Are not your needs met? Rest in peace, Beloved, which is to you both. Amen.

> *Look about you and know the love in what you reflect as pleasing.*

NOVEMBER

CHOOSING LOVE • SPIRIT DIALOG • Monday Evening, November 21

Wow. So much going on and so little time to get it on paper. Can't believe almost a month has gone by since my last writing.

Ray and I are working hard not to fall back into familiar ways and it's coming easy! I can't even begin to get on paper all that we're doing that is so different, but I can honestly say it was worth every bit of the pain and agony of the separation to experience this place, this kind of understanding. Our commitment level is incredible to witness, especially when we get into a tight spot. We're not so eager to throw old shit into what's brewing. If we do and we catch it, whoever tossed it, owns it. If there's a hesitancy to own, there's not a hesitancy to listen to what the other might have to say. Finding this common ground isn't about agreeing to keep the peace. It's about agreeing to discover, dissect, get rid of what doesn't work. And not just for the relationship. It's an amazing balance of honoring our uniqueness as individuals while blending our purpose as a couple. Feels like the perfect fairy tale ending, even though pressures and stresses have not magically disappeared.

My mind just wandered to Sandra and our conversation this morning. She's wrestling. Something is going on with Adam and she won't say what. God, I could feel her pain. It's paradoxical – no, it's twisted that she is even going through something like this. Especially after the part she's played in *our* healing process.

I felt so inadequate talking with her. Nothing she put on me. I just don't want her to hurt, and I don't know what to do to fix that. Ego is telling me I should feel guilty that Ray and I are doing so well. That we don't deserve this if Sandra is suffering. I know the path down which these thoughts will lead me. The very one she worked so hard to boot me off! Would it really make her feel better to watch the unraveling of all the work she supported? Don't think so!

Fear. Guilt. Comparison. Deserve.

Ego. Ego. Ego. And more ego.

I know it's been a long time, guys, but I want your input. Is there something that you can tell me tonight that I could pass on to her that would assist or comfort? What is the loving thing to do, to feel, to share here? Please.

Thank You.

So funny that you see yourself doing for yourself with these writings what you fear you cannot do for others. And yet you have all access to all knowledge, as does Sandra.

It is not the verbiage you seek, but the love behind the verbiage. You feel inadequate not for lack of information, but for your capacity to love. Sandra is given this opportunity to choose love. Not love for Adam but love for Self, as she is able to make the choice to experience herself differently in their relationship. It is no mistake that she be going through these challenges. She has chosen to do so that she might learn to live without the sense of guilt. There are no magic formulas to get her through this time. Indeed, it is the magic that got her in! A different view, a different application is required to move her through the pain.

Sandra's hook is her pain. There is an aspect of self that is deeply invested in the depths to which her pain takes her. You fight us in this, as you write. She romances her pain. It is what grounds her. Tells her she is alive. And so she knows "life" with a little "L." She is as one who says, "Pinch me, so I know I'm not dreaming." A pinch indeed smarts. She is pinching but she is dreaming still. The pain does not make the dream real.

What purpose does her pain fulfill? She may feel it, but she may also choose another function in her pain. Remember when we wrote of confirmation rather than conflagration? And so it can be for Sandra. Let her reflect on her pain and its purpose, but not be trapped by its dictates. She cannot assign the function, but there is One who can. And through this pain she can come to know forgiveness. Where is her investment and why? What does her heart want? Not her head. Not her pain. But her heart, with its new function for pain.

Fear not for Ray or yourself. Yours is still to choose love, and to love when you think to choose fear and all that it would have you do. Every attack can be given another function.

Go in peace and love. You have done well tonight, though much you fight to understand.

Love and Light. Regards to Raymond.

IN THE MARGINS

Thanksgiving has come and gone. There is much to be grateful for. Looking around our "new" home, I see something that wasn't here before: evidence of two very present people. I didn't disappear when Ray's belongings moved back in. Thought he might balk at some of the redecorating I did after he moved out – especially the more feminine touches and brighter colors – but he prefers them. Even my crazy purple door! He says the house feels lighter and that it somehow has given him permission to rethink how he sees himself in the space.

Have adopted the guest room as my personal sanctuary and am really enjoying what I've done with it. He's re-inhabited his office. Having our own space has given us a forum to express, to experience and share, what is different in our tastes. Our bedroom remains as I recreated it – distinctly feminine. A decision we both made. A reminder of the catalyst that created it. Our quirky twist on vulnerability. The rest of the house is becoming an eclectic blend of the two of us. What a curious evolution this has been!

The real work is not in the struggle, but in the careful observation of and accepted responsibility for your creations.

DECEMBER

LAYERS OF LOVE • SPIRIT DIALOG • Sunday, December 4

I woke up this morning with these questions running through my mind. Presented as if they were introduction to a game I should play.

- When I first awake in the morning, before opening my eyes, how do I know who I am? Where I am? What day it is? Or what I awaken to?
- What if I could travel in time, could awake in any morning I desired? Would I know? How do I know I haven't already?

Entertaining these questions has really given me an eerie feeling, guys. Please, explain.

The past and future are but frames you place around the present to make life real. But do you not see that, in doing so, you make the past your present, and the future your past? Was it not an interesting interlude? To question as you lay in bed?

Just think of such possibilities. Were you in bed, without Ray, before or after? Was this a day in the summer when you awakened alone and separated? Was this a day in the future when you awakened alone and reconciled, with a Ray who had just flown to California for a role in a movie? Had you won your lottery months ago? Were paintings in various stages of completion, lining the walls of your studio? What is this present moment?

This contemplation is your door out. Ego frames "now" with past and future, and so you never see the open door through which you will find eternity. They mean nothing, this past present and future past. Frames merely to be manipulated to keep your attention from the door which awaits. Much as the frame you place around a special relationship to keep you from seeing the choice for love within.

When you awaken each morning, continue to use this little game we gave you, and even in some of your waking moments throughout your day. It may be a bit unnerving, but it is necessary for this next growth that you and Ray desire. It is the door through which we reach you. It matters not what you think of any of this.

You seek a happier dream? Then seek it in the present moment. Procrastination is putting off your past, not your future. It is the way you place the past in the future. Yes, it seems it should be the opposite, but it is not. Procrastination insures the past, though it would seem to ward off that which has not yet happened. It concretizes what has always happened.

Just rest and play today. Use this game often. Share it with Ray. Be diligent in this. The lure of the past for you and Ray is as strong as it has ever been. Especially with his confronting his situation created at work. But know that you have chosen this experience to get this message home.

Freedom is now and only now. The more action you take (and your actions are merely symbols of your belief) the more freedom you will know.

Ah, is it not fascinating to be a witness to all this?

Rejoice! Celebrate! You have both done much to heal the world. Though others would not recognize this to be so, it matters not! Go in peace and joy.

Love and Light, dear ones.

IN THE MARGINS

Have been playing this time game, as suggested. Can only do it in small doses. Ray and I both agree it leaves us feeling pretty weird and mildly disoriented. And yet, it invites an odd sort of freedom.

JOURNAL • Wednesday, December 21

Put up our Christmas tree tonight. First in years! A faux tree in a burlap sack. An impulse buy at the art store on one of our artist dates. It is all of eighteen inches high – with *two* trunks. (Which we thought was fittingly symbolic.) Traditional decorations were too big, so we improvised with my dangling earrings and grandma's glass bead necklaces. A vintage scarf from my Mom became a tree skirt and an angel pin, a topper. It might just be the most creative tree we've ever had. Smitty thinks it's the perfect size for him. Will have to find a way to discourage his fascination for my earrings.

Having fun shopping for each other. I am so glad we gave ourselves permission to exchange gifts, in spite of the separation throwing us deeper into debt. What a contrast to recent years when financial obligations and time constraints warranted denying ourselves this holiday tradition – or should I say when we used obligations and constraints to justify our position?

Guess we justified not exchanging gifts by saying that it was more practical – kinder – not to add to our daily stresses with holiday stress. All very true and valid, except in our follow-through. How was it that we managed the time and resources to gift family and friends but not each other? Two creative people who couldn't find a way around those challenges to exchange some token of love for each other? Caught! If we'd had the eyes to see past all our baggage! Sure see it now.

Our funky little tree should be witness to an interesting reflection of what we've learned about love this past year. Loving ourselves and loving each other.

JOURNAL • Monday, December 26

What an awesome Christmas!

Ray presented me with the most incredible gift. Something that perfectly reflects the meaning of this time – with a message I pray we never forget.

One simple little box tied with a big bow. Way out of the budget we had set. Could even say that he had to scrape up everything we had to give it to me! In it was the complete – torn – tattered – scrumpled – scribbled upon copy of *The Artist's Way* that I had all but destroyed and thrown into the box of love trinkets carted out when he left, so many months ago.

I could not believe that he'd kept it. All the pages – pressed – and back in order. God, I could feel the love coming through this man. Past. Present. Future. So many layers. What does one say to that kind of thought? That kind of intention? How many prayers were answered with that one gift?

SPIRIT DIALOG • Wednesday, December 28

The year rounds out to a close, and what an amazing year it has been! Spent some quiet time reading my entries in the journal Lea gave me last Christmas. What a transformation. The past twelve months have taken so many of the issues reflected on those pages and responded to them in very unmistakable, unforgettable ways.

Granted, much appears to be the same. Struggles with creativity and action, financial insecurities, will our arts support us, what to be when we grow up. And yet the core, the ground on which we stand with these issues, has totally shifted.

I lost Ray and found myself – or at least a good start for self. I found myself, and Ray returned.

So is this shift enough to bring about the change in expression that we desire? A year from now, I don't want to be lamenting in my journal about how I am still not expressing, not creating as an artist – and how to change that. All the work that Ray and I have done. I can't stop now. It's not finished.

It is only the setting right of that which needed to be. You fear you will be trapped in this limbo, this struggle you imagine, and yet there is no struggle as you perceive it.

What thought you of that vision yesterday when you looked out to the West upon the sunset and acknowledged a "Bernadette Future" creating at that very instant? And what would she say to you about this "NOW" that you perceive in frustration? The outcome assures itself. She is in joy, so worry not. She assists you even now. Her aspect, this future aspect is, in part, present with us as we share this with you.

You want something concrete, then do something concrete. What have we told you of intentions? Do not let your ego use this as an escape, but you may intend in all you do. Acknowledge "Bernadette Future" and you will find your intentions bringing you ever closer to your desire to express as an artist. This is merely your desire to express God-Self. Your inabilities to create are your guilt and your fears. Guilt for having thrown your God-Self away and fear that in doing so you no longer deserve to be a channel for God's expression. You know you have thrown nothing away, and have nothing to fear. Again a belief in what is not real and what has not happened.

Support will come for you and Ray and when you acknowledge your truth, as we have been showing you, it will come swiftly. Look with humor at your need to imprison. Look to forgiveness. You need no longer the Ray and Bernadette of the past.

Yes, you are worn out with it all. You are a tough customer, but the lesson has finally hit home. So intend in all you do, choose love where're you may, and know that the Spirit of Self is at work in you now.

Ray will be fine if you let him be. You may go through a period of what appears to be lack, but it is merely the last vestiges of an old way and a present opportunity to affirm otherwise. Your beliefs will soon manifest in the form of abundance of projects and the financial means to support them, as well as the energy to back them up.

Is it not amusing, even now as you write, you think you are making this up? And yet you thought the same when we wrote of Ray's return.

February will round out your year and the turning point will occur. First for Ray and then for you, through Ray, in exchange of energies.

All is as it should be, blessed one. Go about your day in peace and love. Allow your Self to greet Ray at the door and call to His. Amen.

> *You seek a happier dream? Then seek it in the present moment. Procrastination is the way you place the past in the future. Procrastination insures the past, though it would seem to ward off that which has not yet happened.*

> *So intend in all you do, choose love where're you may, and know that the Spirit of Self is at work in you now.*

AFTERWARD

And they lived happily ever after. The end.
The end?
So, is it really possible to hold onto that spirit of forgiveness and commitment after the second honeymoon has worn off?
In the debatable glory of the afterglow, this ain't Venus! We are still very much on this planet. The mountains are beautiful to look at from a distance and open to an inspiring panorama from their crest. Climbing them, however, invites an entirely different view. In that climb, there are days when happily-ever-after screams for chucking this relationship into the recycling bin, when the siren voices discredit every conquered peak, every incredible vista shared, and threaten to send us dashing to the rocks below.
Their wales echo, "You prayed for this? What were you thinking? You'll never make it!"
Maybe we won't.
But when the winds whisper of grace, coaxing us off that crumbling ledge, we get to explore the terrain of another beautiful valley – together. Memories, given birth in moments like these, add colors and textures to the heart of an experience that cannot be defined. As we continue to chart our journey through these remote regions, it is comforting to find that they are not the desolate countryside we had feared, but offer incredibly rich landscapes.
Friends and family will testify that our version of happily-ever-after has not been a timid one. Numerous relocations, career shifts, and ongoing financial struggles have put this reconciliation to the test. These challenges could easily have broken us, but when we took the time to run them through the rigors of our

new relationship paradigm, they always led us back to the same crossroads with the same question. What would this moment be like if we let go of fear, let go of guilt, and allowed love to be present?

June of '95 welcomed our twentieth anniversary with a recommitment ceremony that reflected on the miracle of forgiveness. Go back to the dream recorded on May the ninth and you will have the setting. A quaint gardener's cottage nestled at the end of a long winding driveway behind an English Tudor mansion. (Turned out to be the place that Lea was renting at the time.) The outdoor ritual was simple, openly acknowledging our separation and the divine agenda behind it as our strength. Loved ones witnessed our dedication to continuing the healing process and we all celebrated with food and drink under a breezy, blue sky.

October of '96, on Halloween no less, nagging questions about Ray's acting career gave birth to a gypsy lifestyle. Looking for answers, we packed up and headed across country to Los Angeles. This was not a casual decision. We were pulling up stakes and risking everything at a time when things were on the upswing. Ray was back into acting full-time and getting consistently busier. The artist block I'd struggled with had dissolved into a growing passion for sculpting space, resulting in a word of mouth Feng Shui practice. And my production coordinator position had dramatically altered with increased pay, decreased hours, and an assistant.

I could have justifiably (some might say, sensibly) chosen to stay behind while Ray scouted LA. After all, these were his questions. I had his full support in whatever decision I made and absolutely trusted our ability to maintain a long distance relationship. We'd already practiced under the worst of circumstances. This would be a piece of cake! But, having established what good teachers we were for each other, I didn't want to miss anything. It was time to apply all the book knowledge without the safety net of familiar faces and places.

Uncertain about what to expect, we'd decided to yard sale our possessions down to what would fit in a twelve foot truck and ultimately a one bedroom apartment in Los Feliz. If you've ever moved yourself, you know the stress we volunteered for. Our three vehicle, one-car-in-tow caravan was on the road for four days with a very vocal Smitty the kitty, loudly questioning our sanity.

Just five months after arriving in LA, I started getting nudges to pull together this book. This was not a new thought. Shortly after we reconciled, I shared some of these pages with Ray. (I had been curious about their accuracy concerning what had taken place on his side of the fence.) Amazed, he confirmed many hits and made the comment that I had "a book in there," leaving me with a very odd feeling. When flashes started coming to *write the book*, I pushed them aside, arguing that I had all I could handle in adjusting to the challenges this new city presented. The creative process of writing a safely fictional and anonymous story was beyond me. An electrical charge ran through my body when, one day, the words shot back, *"What is your problem? We've already written half of it for you!"*

When the *pull it together as is* implication sank in, all I could think was, "Oh my God, I can't do this. You can't ask me to be that vulnerable." To which they replied, *"We're not asking you. You've already agreed to this."*

I slowly started the task of gathering and organizing. Struggling with the degree of personal exposure confronting me and debating that a journal format would not be fair to Ray's side of the story. I sensed *their* amusement when he offered to input the material I had gathered thus far, freeing me to edit.

Bless his heart! He typed all the pages I hadn't shared with him. All that dreadful hurt and anger. And the worst of it (March and April) while I was back east facilitating, oddly enough, a series of relationship workshops with Sandra. Alone at the keyboard, alternating feelings of gratitude and guilt kept him company. One evening, while we were chatting on the phone, he confessed to feeling overwhelmed at what an out-of-touch-asshole he had been. There I was, confronted with the ultimate temptation and pay-back fantasy. An opportunity to twist the knife. Instead, I found myself blurting out, "Don't you *dare* pick up the guilt. You did what was necessary so we could learn to release it and I am grateful. This book is not about inviting it back in." In that moment, I witnessed the legacy of those pages.

Flashes about a *sign of fire and water* continued for many months after the journal entry, dated June the twenty-sixth. Not having gotten a direct answer, I felt that the sign connected to a place in the mountains where Ray and I would be spending time. Of course in relating to Atlanta, I was thinking The Blue Ridge. I was a little off on my geographic impression. July of '98, four years and one month later, sitting outside a little French cafe in Glendale, California with mountain ranges all around, the answer finally came.

Sandra had flown out for a visit. We'd decided to have dinner at this little cafe and were sitting outside, so she and Ray could smoke. Ray had just lit up a cigar, when a couple sat down next to us. Mind you, this was the smoking section and we were sitting at the only table taken, on the far corner. There were at least a dozen other tables available. The woman became very huffy and made a production out of calling the waiter and moving their utensils and menus to another table. As her agitation continued to be apparent, I could feel Ray's heat rise. He is a considerate smoker and was making a point of drafting his smoke away from them. I started trying to smooth things over with him before he even acknowledged irritation at her attitude. This did not go well. We started a politely intense, and far too familiar, tug of war. We were well into it by the time the couple moved to a table inside. Apparently the cafe could not serve alcohol on the patio and she wanted a drink. God bless that woman and the angels using her.

Silently waiting for her moment, Sandra smiled slyly and said, "I bet this has been happening a lot." Stunned by the accuracy of her comment, she had our full attention. As she started into her story about fire and water and a pot, I knew this was the *pay attention* sign that my angels had given me so long ago.

She went on to ask, "What happens to a pot of water when the flame is turned up?"

"It evaporates." We answered.

She continued, "What happens to fire when water spills over?"

"It's extinguished." We replied.

With Ray as fire and me as water, we got a quick picture of what was at stake when we argued. Sure extinction for both! When uncomfortable or challenged, I use water to level out and cool down. Ray uses fire to rise up and blow off. My invisibility issues and his respect issues, coupled with our misapplied corrections, always guaranteed one hell of a fight for survival.

The metal pot, representing our creativity, allows us to coexist. Its shape, forged from fire and cooled by water, produces a useful object. This is what Ray and I share when honoring our creative spirits. This is what makes our fire and water work. The *sign of fire and water* is a tool we use to this day.

Somewhere, between the everyday Los Angeles experiences and explorations, this book found its passage into the world. Busy at the computer, in our little kitchen on the sixth floor, I found myself glancing up as the sun faded into the horizon, casting its coral hue on the city – and across my keyboard. I had just finished typing these words from the page dated December the twenty-eighth.

"*What thought you of that vision yesterday, when you looked out to the West, and upon the sunset, and acknowledged a 'Bernadette Future' creating at that very instant! And what would she say to you about this 'NOW' that you perceive in frustration? The outcome assures itself. She assists you even now."*

Tears streamed down my face as I felt my spirit fold over time like the wrinkle of a garment. Under divine guidance, I was now "Bernadette Future" *creating at that very instant*, and the process of birthing this book was somehow assisting our past. Beyond my understanding and needing only my acceptance, these pages were bread crumbs left behind, leading the way on a strangely familiar trail. Evidence of help at hand.

Not long after completing the bulk of this manuscript, Ray's questions were answered. Soul searching the root of his creative drive as an actor had revealed and liberated a fine artist within. And though the Los Angeles quest officially initiated as his, the West had given me a few answers of my own. The part-time Feng Shui practice that I started before leaving Atlanta anchored in as my life's work. My creative drive as an artist found its expression. Working one-on-one to create supportive environments – especially with women going through their own life changing transitions – became my passion. "Enlightened Interiors" was born.

With three rainbows and our angels' blessings, we decided to move back to Atlanta. This time we did not move ourselves. And this time Smitty was silent. He knew he was going home.

We perched in an apartment for six months, scouting the area for a little house to rent. Found one a few miles up the road from my purple door. (Which was now painted green.) Continuing to be driven by our passions and creativity, the joke was that we were still living in a gypsy's wagon. The only difference being that now we had a bigger rock under the wheel and an agreement that I got the next kick.

Our twenty-sixth anniversary found me unexpectedly kicking that rock out from under as we purchased our very own fixer-upper back in Covington. The place where the Shelly seed was planted. Vacant and full of debris, an old mill house welcomed us home, removing all doubt with the front page from a discarded newspaper, neatly folded on the living room floor next to a tattered leather recliner. The date? March 3. Where these pages began. Full circle!

Looking out our bedroom window each morning, we are greeted by a huge tree. At first glance it appears to be one. But as we look up toward the heavens the branches reveal two species of leaves. Two trees. One trunk. Roots intermingled. Intimately drawing nourishment from the same source. Yet maintaining their uniqueness.

Life is never boring as we continue to be intrigued and humbled by what we share. Not held fast by the trappings of hearts and flowers, but by the integrity of a relationship that seems to have a life of its own. A relationship that insists we honor each other as lover *and* teacher. Better than we knew, bigger than the experiences we find ourselves in, and guided by God.

I asked Ray if he would be willing to give voice to his side here – to what got this whole thing in motion. I'll leave you with his words.

"I prayed to be shown what love was. For my heart to open. I believed Shelly was God's answer. She was. I had to be shown what love wasn't. When I understood that, I found you in my heart."

Amen! And God bless!